Cambridge Elements

Elements in Contentious Politics
edited by
David S. Meyer
University of California, Irvine
Suzanne Staggenborg
University of Pittsburgh

THE JENA 6

Of Nooses, Fights, Narratives, and Movement Building

Pamela Oliver
University of Wisconsin–Madison

Chaeyoon Lim
Washington University in St Louis

Anna Milewski
University of Wisconsin–Madison

Erin Gaede
University of Wisconsin–Madison

CAMBRIDGE
UNIVERSITY PRESS

Shaftesbury Road, Cambridge CB2 8EA, United Kingdom

One Liberty Plaza, 20th Floor, New York, NY 10006, USA

477 Williamstown Road, Port Melbourne, VIC 3207, Australia

314–321, 3rd Floor, Plot 3, Splendor Forum, Jasola District Centre,
New Delhi – 110025, India

Cambridge University Press is part of Cambridge University Press & Assessment,
a department of the University of Cambridge.

We share the University's mission to contribute to society through the pursuit of
education, learning and research at the highest international levels of excellence.

www.cambridge.org
Information on this title: www.cambridge.org/9781009669030

DOI: 10.1017/9781009669009

When citing this work, please include a reference to the DOI 10.1017/9781009669009

First published 2026

A catalogue record for this publication is available from the British Library

*A Cataloging-in-Publication data record for this Element is available from
the Library of Congress*

ISBN 978-1-009-66903-0 Hardback
ISBN 978-1-009-66902-3 Paperback
ISSN 2633-3570 (online)
ISSN 2633-3562 (print)

Additional resources for this publication at www.cambridge.org/Oliver.

Cambridge University Press & Assessment has no responsibility for the persistence
or accuracy of URLs for external or third-party internet websites referred to in this
publication and does not guarantee that any content on such websites is, or will remain,
accurate or appropriate.

For EU product safety concerns, contact us at Calle de José Abascal, 56, 1°, 28003
Madrid, Spain, or email eugpsr@cambridge.org

The Jena 6

Of Nooses, Fights, Narratives, and Movement Building

Elements in Contentious Politics

DOI: 10.1017/9781009669009
First published online: April 2026

Pamela Oliver
University of Wisconsin–Madison

Chaeyoon Lim
Washington University in St Louis

Anna Milewski
University of Wisconsin–Madison

Erin Gaede
University of Wisconsin–Madison

Author for correspondence: Pamela Oliver, pamela.oliver@wisc.edu

Abstract: Tens of thousands of mostly younger Black people went to rural Louisiana in 2007 to support the Jena 6, Black students who were overcharged after a school fight. We examine the construction of two narratives. The powerful Jena 6 narrative told how the conflict began when nooses were hung on the school grounds, linking historic racial violence to modern injustice. This narrative emphasized student agency and downplayed documented adult actions. A second narrative about organizing the campaign incorrectly said that existing organizations had ignored the case. We use published sources to trace the ordinary processes as activists, journalists, and organizations became involved in the campaign through three phases – regional organizing, nationalization, scale shift to cascade. In the last phase, many saw this as a historic reinvigoration of the Black movement. Circulating narratives inspired participation by stressing youthful agency and spontaneity. More accurate accounts are better for theory and action.

Keywords: African American history, social movements, criminal justice, Protest, Black history

ISBNs: 9781009669030 (HB), 9781009669023 (PB), 9781009669009 (OC)
ISSNs: 2633-3570 (online), 2633-3562 (print)

Contents

An Online Appendix for this Element is available at
www.cambridge.org/Oliver

Introduction

On September 20, 2007, tens of thousands of Black people from around the United States protested in the small town of Jena in rural Louisiana. Tens of thousands more protested in solidarity around the country. Organizations across the Black political spectrum came, including SCLC, NAACP, NAN, Nation of Islam, Malcolm X Grassroots Movement, New Black Panther Party, student groups, labor unions, fraternities and sororities, motorcycle clubs, and churches. Al Sharpton, Jesse Jackson, and Martin Luther King III were there, as were national Black radio hosts Michael Baisden and Tom Joyner, rap music stars, and many other Black celebrities and politicians. At the time, it was seen as a possible regeneration of the Black movement. Most attendees were young, and Black newspapers celebrated the entry of a new generation into the movement. This was one of the first large Black protests of the Internet age. Advance communication about the case circulated primarily through Black channels including Black radio, blogs, Facebook, email, and Black newspapers. Activists organized follow-up events and sought to build a movement around the enthusiasm it generated. Some speculate that the energy it generated helped to elect President Obama or that it was the beginning of the activism that later escalated into Black Lives Matter.

The Jena 6[1] protests were covered in thousands of news stories in 2007 that offered varying versions of the story of a racist small town where first White students hung nooses on a tree in an area traditionally reserved for Whites after Black students sat (or asked to sit) there, and then six Black students were charged with attempted murder after the beating of a White student. On its face, the attempted murder charge was excessive. The victim, while knocked unconscious and injured, was released from the hospital in a few hours and attended an event that evening. The accused teens were threatened with decades in prison for what many viewed as an ordinary fight. The case resonated with Black Americans because it linked racial violence and lynching symbolized by nooses with racial discrimination in the criminal justice system. The protest itself became a historic event people wanted to experience.

There are two narratives about the Jena 6 case. One is what happened in Jena about the noose-hanging and the fight, and the attributions made about the relations between events. We were first drawn to this story because the inconsistencies in the many news articles about the case offered a case study in narrative construction. In this Element, we compare the events documented in contemporaneous and early sources with those that circulated later with a focus

---

[1] Both "Jena Six" and "Jena 6" were used to name the protests. We generally use "Jena 6" because this was the more common choice in Black sources.

on which acts of collective resistance were and were not part of the Jena 6 narrative as it circulated.

As we dug into the case, we found a second narrative had been constructed about how the campaign grew. The *New York Times* and other elite "national" news sources did not cover the story until a few days before the big protest and many writers faulted the "mainstream media" for ignoring the story (e.g., Christie 2008). Writers said bloggers "sounded the alarm" (Kvasny, Payton, and Hales 2009) and said a "formidable grassroots organization" and "viral civil rights movement" was "literally conjured out of the ether of cyberspace and spread via blogs, e-mail, message boards and Black radio" (Witt 2007a). These accounts also are inconsistent, naming different people or groups as starting the movement. Only a handful mentioned claims that Ernest Johnson of the Louisiana NAACP and Alan Bean's Friends of Justice had been working in Jena all along. This led us to search for more information.

In this Element, we take a process tracing approach using multiple sources to piece together who got involved when and comparing that with quantitative measures of news coverage and public attention. We identify three phases of the campaign – regional organizing, nationalization, and the communications and participation cascade – and discuss the transitions between the phases. We compare evidence about how and when the campaign grew with the circulating narratives. Contrary to those who argued that the case should have been a big story sooner or that the outcome was an inevitable result of the power of the Jena 6 narrative, we argue that the scale shift happened when national activists saw an opportunity for movement building.

In both cases, our primary sources are news articles and other published materials supplemented by a few interviews with activists and journalists[2] and quantitative analyses of mainstream and Black news coverage and Google trends. We did not attempt an ethnographic study of Jena. Although we began with questions about the role of bloggers, most of the blogs and social media posts from that time are unavailable. We are aware of these limitations and seek to write carefully about what we can and cannot know from our sources. We show that the available news articles themselves provide the basis for more complex accounts than the narratives the news articles offered.

This Element has six major sections after this introduction. The first section outlines the theoretical arguments and provides an overview of the Jena story. The second section discusses what happened in Jena with the nooses and the fight in the fall of 2006 and what was included and not included in the narratives

---

[2] Those we interviewed, all White, responded to email inquiries within a few days, typically within a few hours. We had no contact information for some individuals, and emails sent to others were never answered.

about this case as it circulated. We show that the changes in the narrative over time increasingly emphasized young people's resistance and downplayed the broader context of adult conflict and actions.

The third section focuses on the growth of the Jena 6 campaign. We identify three phases: regional organizing, nationalization, and media-mobilization cascade. We trace its prosaic development as people worked through ordinary channels involving activists and journalists and their personal and organizational networks. We compile evidence about exactly when the scale shift from ordinary mobilizing to cascade happened and argue that the cascade was spurred by a movement-building impulse. The fourth section discusses the September rally itself including evidence of the role of on-the-ground groups in getting people to Jena, what happened there, the movement building efforts that were tied to it, and how the protest was discussed in mainstream and Black news sources.

The fifth section provides a brief overview of the aftermath of the campaign and the sixth and final section offers some reflections on the implications of the case. Online Appendix A provides a timeline and list of names; Appendix B summarizes other academic research on the topic and lists blogs and news articles consulted. Appendix C analyzes the content of news coverage of Jena events, Appendix D inventories buses that went to Jena, and Appendix E analyzes trends in news coverage and Google searches. Additional information including links to videos about the case is available on the first author's blog.[3]

1 Movement Narratives and Movement Realities

There are different threads of social movements writing using the broad concept of "narrative." One thread emphasizes the importance of stories about the movement for recruiting participants, inspiring action, and claiming credit. Writing thirty years ago, Gamson (1995) identified three aspects of collective action frames – injustice (moral indignation), agency (possible to do something), and identity (a we-ness, we will make change) – and stressed the importance of bridging the abstract and the concrete to generate a sense of agency. Similarly, Fine (1995) found three kinds of narratives told by movement activists: horror stories that justify the movement, war stories spurring individuals to participate, and happy endings function as morale boosters. Couto (1993) describes how narratives about the Civil Rights Movement from four rural communities fostered memories of past repression and resistance. Polletta (1998b, 1998a) shows how narratives of spontaneity that downplayed the role

---

[3] www.ssc.wisc.edu/soc/racepoliticsjustice/

of prior organization helped to create student activist as an identity and make high-risk activism attractive.

We show that the circulating narratives about the Jena 6 emphasized young people's resistance to racism in challenging segregation at school, being met with nooses, and protesting the nooses. The school fight itself was often constructed as an act of resistance to racial slurs and even, in some versions, as resistance to the nooses. For example, Florini (2012, 2014) analyzed the Malcolm X Grassroots Movement webpage's coverage of the Jena case, finding that it interpreted Jena as part of a Black Power narrative, as self-defense in an environment of terror.

Meyer (2006) emphasizes the importance of movement narratives in claiming credit for movement success, and the ways in which different accounts have different implications for both understanding how movements work and for recruiting future participants. In the buildup to the big September rally, the main movement narratives involved the relatively spontaneous uprising of Black people via blogs, Black radio, Internet email campaigns or social media. As the rally came together, radio host Michael Baisden and Black activist Al Sharpton were most often mentioned in news media.

After the big rally, there were more claims about who deserved credit for the Jena campaign. Michael Baisden claimed credit for getting people to Jena. Alan Bean claimed credit for the media campaign. Some opponents flipped Bean's claim to blame him for concocting a false story. Academics and many news accounts credited Black media and social media, especially bloggers, radio hosts, and ColorOfChange.org for communicating the media message when mainstream media was ignoring it. The NAACP highlighted its early involvement.

The other main line of work using the narrative concept is process tracing, where analysts seek to explain outcomes by tracing how events connect to each other (Abell 2004). In this approach, an explanation for why things happened is how they happened. We explain the big Jena rally and wave of solidarity rallies and broad support for the mobilization by tracing how and when the campaign built. We find that the movement mobilization happened in three phases. The first phase of regional activism and the second stage of expanding national support followed the lines of an ordinary protest campaign as support gradually built through multiple channels of publicity and prior personal and organizational network ties. We draw brief comparisons with other cases of injustice to a Black youth that were in the news at the same time.

The third phase is a relatively sudden shift to a communication and mobilization cascade in the three weeks before the big rally. Our findings suggest that the entry of Black radio hosts into the campaign fueled the cascade and that the cascade's energy arose from the campaign's perceived importance as a historic moment in Black history. In discussing all three phases, we stress the importance of existing groups and activists and on-the-ground actions alongside media and social media campaigns. We also point to the distinct threads of organizing and motivations among those who made the Jena 6 campaign happen.

Prosaic Non-Romantic Narratives about Movements

Narratives of spontaneity like Rosa Parks just being tired and the #BlackLivesMatter hashtag starting a movement are central to popular understandings of protest. While narratives of spontaneity can inspire action and aid recruitment, real-life collective action happens through more prosaic and probabilistic channels. Narratives of spontaneity tell only success stories, but in real life, most instances of collective action against oppression fail or have only limited impact. Many supporters of the Jena 6 complained that mainstream media and national Black organizations ignored the Jena 6 case, believing the case should have been treated as important sooner. But there are many cases of injustice and only a few can become major national issues. We flip the question around: why in this case was there the exceptional outcome of a huge mass mobilization and, in consequence, a media and participation cascade?

National mainstream media ignore most cases of injustice partly because there are literally too many cases of injustice to fit in the news. Before the Internet, there were physical limitations, often called "news holes," of available column inches in newspapers or minutes in television news broadcasts. Editors chose what to put in and inevitably a lot was left out. Even with seemingly unlimited space for information on the Internet, there are still finite limits to human attention. Only a few stories can be "top stories." This means that every potential news story competes for public attention with every other potential news story.

It is difficult to build a large movement around cases of legal injustice. The Black Lives Movement focused on police killings, but even for police killings, most cases are not protested. Protests typically occur only when the victim was doing nothing illegal or threatening and the officers engaged in gross misconduct (Burch 2023; Lawrence 2000; Lu 2024). Even when there are local protests, most are covered in only a few local news stories. Very few cases ever become big national news stories.

The Jena 6 case involved overcharging. There was a victim: Justin Barker had been beaten. There were ambiguities about who did it, what their motivations were, what the context was, and how serious his injuries were. Advocates believed that the attempted murder charges were unreasonable and racially discriminatory. But it was never a simple case of complete innocence of everyone charged. It is difficult to build a major protest movement around such a case, regardless of where it occurs.

In fact, another case of overcharging a Black youth was in the news in 2007. In December 2006, Genarlow Wilson was sentenced to ten years in prison for being the recipient of consensual oral sex from a girl two years younger than he was. Before August 2007, the Wilson case received more coverage in both Black and mainstream news outlets than the Jena case.[4] Both the NAACP and Al Sharpton were advocating around the Wilson case, and ColorOfChange.org was featuring it on its website before switching to Jena in mid-July. It is even possible that the Wilson case was competing with the Jena case for attention from national media and organizations. But the Wilson case never turned into a major media cascade.

That is where the nooses came in. The Jena 6 narrative linked hanging nooses in response to a challenge to segregation to the later overcharging of Black youths in a fight, powerfully tying a history of racial violence and terror to injustice in the criminal legal system. The nooses became central to motivating the protest wave (Greenlea 2014).

Important as the nooses and the noose-fight narrative were, however, they did not immediately provoke large-scale collective action, nor was the narrative itself some kind of magical agent. Although the noose-fight narrative began circulating in May 2007, the energy and organization around the case began building only after Mychal Bell's guilty verdict at the end of June and did not turn into a cascade until September. We show that, although amplification through social media mattered, the work around constructing and deploying the narrative and using it to mobilize action largely happened through prosaic channels of media coverage, existing organizations, and prior network ties. We find multiple paths of influence that reinforced each other with positive feedbacks as newer Internet-based communication operated alongside older radio communication to spread the message in a more decentralized way.

It was not enough to spread the message about injustice. Large-scale collective action also involves solving the mundane problems around transportation, agendas, coordination, and clean-up – what we might think of as "movement housework." Physical human beings do this work in physical places. The big rally and the solidarity rallies around the country were organized on the ground by place-based groups. The existence and actions of these place-based networks and groups is an important part of the whole story that has been largely

---

[4] See Appendix E or www.ssc.wisc.edu/soc/racepoliticsjustice/2025/06/18/news-coverage-of-the-jena-6/.

neglected in popular narratives and most academic accounts of the Jena 6 campaign, with the exceptions of Greenlea (2014) and (Flaherty 2010).

National and Local Movement Organizations

The contrast between the spontaneity and cyberspace narratives and our process tracing narrative reveals important lessons to be learned from the Jena mobilization. Many criticized national-level movement organizations for being slow to pick up the Jena case. But just as with the media, it is impossible for national organizations to give the highest possible attention to every local case of injustice. Instead, national organizations such as the NAACP and ACLU have a federated structure in which local groups work on local issues. Local NAACP chapters played a crucial role in addressing local cases of injustice during the Civil Rights Era (Current 1988) and after 1965 (Minchin 2008). Many communities also have other local organizations that address local issues. Regional representatives of the NAACP, ACLU, and NAN were all present in Jena in the first half of 2007. The Jena 6 case got picked up by national Black organizations after Mychal Bell's conviction at the end of June 2007 revealed that regional support was not sufficient.

Little has been written theorizing the relationships between local and national campaigns and movements, although the case study literature is full of examples. Historical accounts of the Civil Rights movement describe local activists who led local campaigns and interacted with "outside" movements and activists (e.g., Payne 1995; Morris 1984; Robnett 1997; Kelley 2015). Similarly, the recent Black Lives Movement built on longstanding local organizations and campaigns that were connected to each other and to national networks and organizations (Oliver 2020; Taylor 2016; Ransby 2018). The specific approach of publicizing cases of unjust prosecution to draw outside attention and to pressure local authorities was used by the Communist-led International Labor Defense of the early 1930s, most famously around the Scottsboro case (Kelley 2015, 78–91) which the Southern Negro Youth Congress sought to emulate in 1940 (Kelley 2015, 316). These campaigns simultaneously sought to redress cases of injustice and to build a movement.

Many studies recognize that the needs and agendas of local groups are often different from or in tension with the needs and agendas of national or transnational groups (e.g., Bob 2002; Vanderkooy and Nawyn 2011; Friedman 2009; Ehrhardt 2020; Oliver and Furman 1989; Marquez 2021). Local organizing for local needs is different from mobilizing for large mass protests (Voss and Williams 2012). Local campaigns can benefit from broader visibility and resources provided by national or international organizations, while national or international organizations often choose specific local cases strategically for their value in building support for themselves (e.g., Morris 1984; Rothman and Oliver 1999; Rootes 2013). National-level organizations often try to build a more sustained national-level movement from the energy and attention generated by a case that has attracted attention, as happened in 2014 after the police killings of Eric Garner in New York and Michael Brown in Ferguson and again in 2020 after the killing of George Floyd in Minneapolis. This is what we find as the Jena campaign unfolded.

Different Movement Networks

In addition to the national-local dimension, broadly allied movements differentiate horizontally in their foci and constituencies. Reuning and Banaszak (2020) helpfully argue that protests have different kinds of goals which they typologize as directly producing change, indirectly producing change by changing narratives, and building a movement or community. Broadly, the Jena campaign involved two movement networks that emphasized different goals.

One network included Alan Bean and his Friends of Justice, the ACLU, and other activist networks centered in Louisiana and Texas. This network focused primarily on addressing the legal problems of the Jena 6. As Alan Bean said often, the goal was to pressure local authorities and persuade large law firms to provide pro bono legal counsel.[5] These regional legal activists were linked to broader regional networks of progressive activists and journalists who, in turn, were linked to national networks of progressive activists and journalists. These activists and journalists were primarily White but included key Black actors as well. White journalists who provided early coverage mostly communicated with these activists and focused primarily on the legal case.

The other network was primarily focused on movement building, specifically on building a Black movement that would have the collective power to address the concerns of Black people generally, including the broad problems of injustice in the criminal legal system. Campaigns about specific issues were viewed in part as means to the larger end of movement building. This included the NAACP and its regional chapters, Al Sharpton and the local chapters of his National Action Network, other civil rights groups, the Nation of Islam and its political arm the Millions More Movement, and other Black organizations. It also included Black bloggers and Black radio hosts. These groups connected with Black churches and school and community groups that provided the grassroots infrastructure for the mobilization. Greenlea's (2014) research on

---

[5] See Boutcher (2013) for the importance of large law firms in "cause" and legal aid lawyering.

the Jena 6 case emphasizes the formation of Black collective identity as central to the mobilization.

Both networks were active from the beginning. Even though they differed in emphasis, both networks combined concern about the Jena 6 themselves with movement-building goals. The two movement networks interacted and reinforced each other. The activists and journalists in the legal network got the message out and brought in mainstream media coverage and outside pressure that succeeded in drawing in pro bono legal help for the Jena 6. Black activists organized the upswelling of Black collective action around the case that drew participants to the September 20 rally.

After September 20, the work of the legal activist network was mostly done, except for continuing to monitor the legal developments until the case was resolved, while the Black movement activists sought to convert the Jena 6 momentum into a reinvigorated Black movement.

News Media and Social Media

Part of the Jena story is how the message got out. Academic researchers often focus narrowly on the *New York Times* and other elite national-level newspapers, and protesters at the time complained about the failure of the *New York Times* and other "national" newspapers to cover the Jena case. We find that the Jena 6 case was covered in other mainstream news sources. There has also been a flurry of relatively recent research on first Facebook and then Twitter, largely because the data could be easily downloaded. But other media channels matter, even though they are less easily studied, and different media channels have been important for different movements and in different eras.

Commentators at the time called out the importance of Black radio for the Jena 6 campaign and our process tracing supports radio as important in the third phase of the campaign. Radio is an under-studied communication channel, largely because there are no readily accessible data archives. The most economically viable sector of radio in the United States is talk radio (Berry and Sobieraj 2011), which engages listeners through call-ins, so that it takes on the character of a conversation or forum. Tom Joyner's morning show and Michael Baisden's afternoon show were four-hour blocks that interwove Black-oriented music with conversation about a wide variety of topics, including Black political issues (di Leonardo 2012). Each had about eight million listeners (Greenlea 2014, 130–141). Tyree and Williams (2024) report that radio still reaches over 90% of Black people monthly and say, "At its core, Black radio remains a vital information source for the engagement of Black audiences in civic engagement, community building, economic education and empowerment, health education, political activism, and the dissemination of vital cultural knowledge" (Tyree and Williams 2024, 8). Although most White-centric talk radio is dominated by conservatives (Mayer 2004; Mort 2012), there are progressive broadcast communication channels, especially Democracy Now and programming on National Public Radio and the Public Broadcasting System. Our process tracing identified progressive alternative media as significant in the Jena 6 case. We expect that different specialized media will be important for different movements.

We devoted effort to a largely unsuccessful attempt to weigh the impact of bloggers in the Jena campaign. In 2007, social media was still new and there was popular and academic interest in its significance. Legacy newspapers were collapsing in the wake of lost ad revenue from the spread of Craigslist in the 2000s (Djourelova, Durante, and Martin 2025). Both journalists who still had jobs and those who had been laid off were looking for new ways to reach audiences. Bloggers and things called blogs were diverse, ranging from the websites of print and broadcast news organizations to online-only news and commentary sites to institutional and academic sites publishing long-form essays and research to individuals writing personal essays to individuals who wrote microblogs that linked to things written by others, sometimes with short comments attached. Facebook became open to anyone with an email address in September 2006 and its user base was growing rapidly in 2007. Unfortunately, the vast majority of blog and social media posts from 2007 are no longer accessible and it is impossible from this distance to provide any reliable assessment of the impact of bloggers relative to other sources of communication. Our best estimate is that blogging amplified and ran parallel to rather than leading legacy media.

2 What Happened in Jena?

After setting the context, this section discusses the construction of the various narratives about events in Jena in the fall of 2006 and shows how the circulating narratives emphasized young people's collective resistance.

Jena and Its Context

Jena is a small town (population 3,317 in 2010) that is the parish seat and largest incorporated place in rural LaSalle Parish (population 15,000) in central Louisiana. Parish officials made the infamous decisions in the Jena case. Jena High School, one of two in the parish, is governed by the LaSalle Parish school board and school superintendent. LaSalle Parish District Attorney J. Reed Walters was the prosecutor. LaSalle Parish is one of the wealthiest in

Louisiana, partly due to oil reserves. It was 85% White and 12% Black in 2010, much Whiter than Louisiana as a whole, which was 32% Black in 2010. It had a high level of donation to Republican candidates and a reputation as a KKK area due in part to high vote totals for former KKK leader David Duke in the 1990 gubernatorial election.

The unincorporated area outside the Jena town limits is called "Ward 10" in news stories about the Jena 6. Ward 10 of LaSalle Parish overlaps substantially (but not entirely) with Midway, a Census designated unincorporated place. Figure 1 shows the boundaries of Jena and Midway and the locations of key events in the Jena 6 story. In 2010, over half (57%) of the Black residents of LaSalle Parish lived in the combined Jena-Midway area versus only 26% of the White LaSalle Parish residents. The town limits of Jena are drawn so that in 2010 it was 84% White and 11% Black. In 2010, Midway's population of 1,297 was 42% White, 50% Black, and 7% American Indian. The Jena band of the Choctaw has offices in Trout, about four miles west of Jena on US highway 84. Of the combined population of Jena plus Midway, 93% of the American Indian people and 65% of the Black people lived in Midway versus only 16.5% of the White people. The only Black member of the LaSalle Parish school board represented Ward 10 and lived in Midway. The boys who became the Jena 6 lived in Ward 10. The two Black churches named as sites of organizing were both in the unincorporated area outside the Jena town limits, as was Good Pine Middle School, where a July 2007 forum attended by Black residents was held.

Jena High School had about 500 students and was about 10% Black. It served surrounding rural areas as well as Jena and Ward 10/Midway. High school was the first experience with integration for many White students at Jena High School. Accounts in news stories imply that Jena was like much of the United States in being legally integrated and informally segregated. The racial attitudes of individual White people varied, with overt White supremacists being part of the mix while others were more egalitarian. There were two Black teachers at Jena High and there were student and adult friendships across racial lines, even as there was a general pattern of social segregation and White political, economic, and social domination.

The Jena Juvenile Detention center was opened in 1998 and closed in 2000 after advocacy by the Juvenile Justice Project of Louisiana about abusive treatment by corrections staff of Black and Latino youth. It reopened in 2005 to house incarcerated evacuees after hurricane Katrina, and there were reports of abusive and racist treatment of the evacuees by correctional officers. It was closed during the Jena 6 events. In October 2007, the facility reopened as the LaSalle ICE Processing Center and is in the news in 2025 as the Central Louisiana ICE Processing Center where immigrants are being detained.

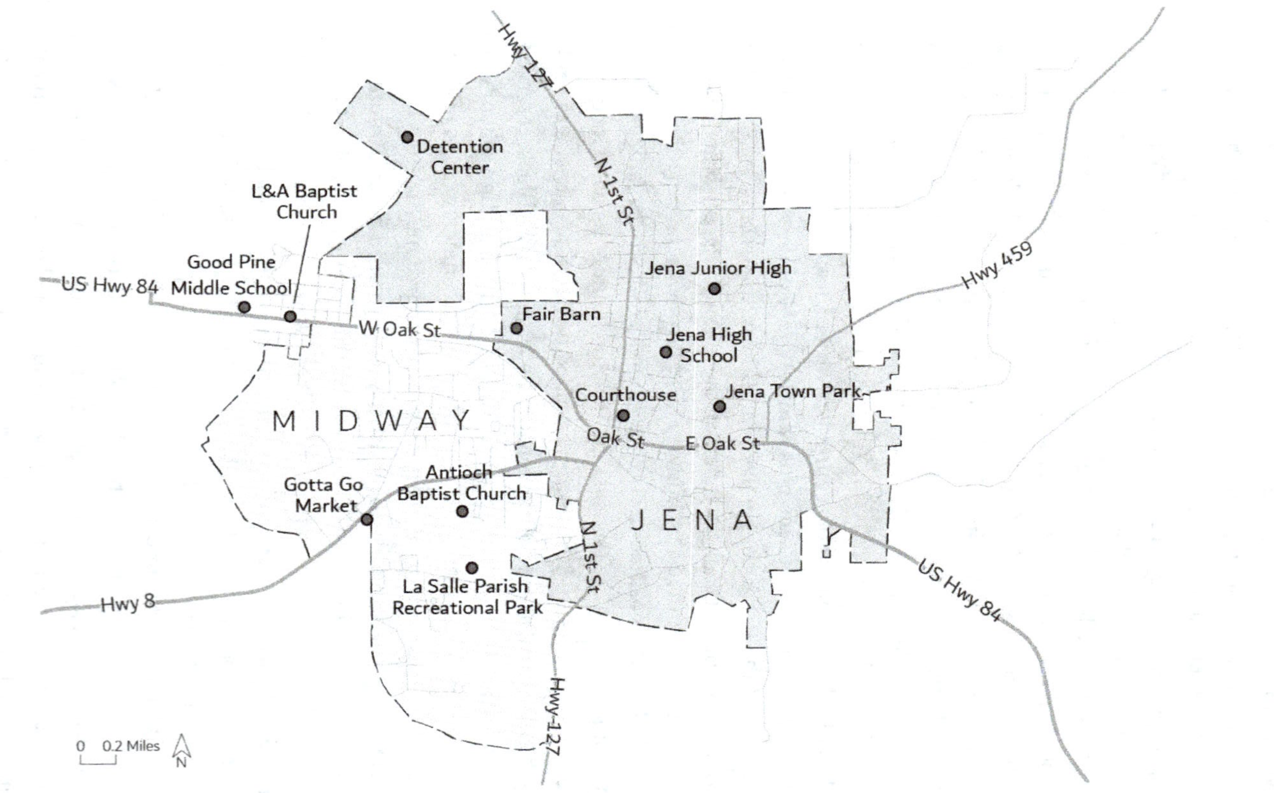

Figure 1 Map of Town of Jena and unincorporated Midway, Louisiana, showing sites of events mentioned in this Element. Map by Anya Shaw.

Jena is relatively isolated in a hilly wooded region where the primary industry is timber. As the map in Figure 2 shows, it is served only by two-lane roads. It is forty miles from Interstate 49 at Alexandria. Alexandria and its twin city Pineville combined had about 63,000 residents in 2007. The next nearest city is Monroe, 65 miles away in the opposite direction, population 50,000. Larger cities are more than a hundred miles away.

Alexandria is important in this story. The Alexandria city government officially welcomed the Jena protesters in September 2007 and Alexandria was the staging area for the Jena protest. Its newspaper, radio stations, and television station serve the Central Louisiana area and covered the nooses and the Jena 6 case. Alexandria's population was and is over half Black. Pineville, across the river from Alexandria, is majority White but elected a Black mayor in 2000 who served for more than twenty years. Alexandria's first Black mayor was elected in 2018. There are two colleges in the area, the Alexandria branch of Louisiana State University, and the private Baptist-affiliated Louisiana College.

The Jena 6 Narrative

The Jena 6 were Black teens charged with attempted murder after the beating of White fellow Jena High student Justin Barker on December 4, 2007: Mychal Bell (the only one who went to trial and was convicted), Robert Bailey, Jr., Theo Shaw, Carwin Jones, Bryant Purvis, and Jesse Beard.

The Jena 6 narrative connected a noose-hanging that occurred on September 1, 2006, with a fight that occurred three months later. Alan Bean has often recounted the story of creating the narrative and recruiting journalists to cover it (Bean 2009, 2010; Greenlea 2014, 39–40). The Jena 6 story was not fiction: the events happened. But it "connected the narrative dots" (Bean 2009) between the noose-hanging and the fight to tell a story of how "one thing led to another" (Bean 2010). Bean's goal was to get outside media attention for small town cases typically ignored by the national press to pressure local authorities and attract pro bono legal support from high profile firms. A press briefing with an event list was circulated by email; a copy was posted by a blogger on April 10, 2007 (McCoy 2007) and on Bean's Friends of Justice website on June 12, 2007 (FOJ 06–12). We refer to this document below as Bean's event list.

The framework for the circulating narrative was provided by three articles published in May 2007. Bean recruited two journalists whose pieces appeared on May 20, 2007, pegged to the original trial date for two of the boys: Tom Mangold's BBC documentary and accompanying blog post, and Howard Witt's *Chicago Tribune* article. Louisiana ACLU activist Tory Pegram recruited

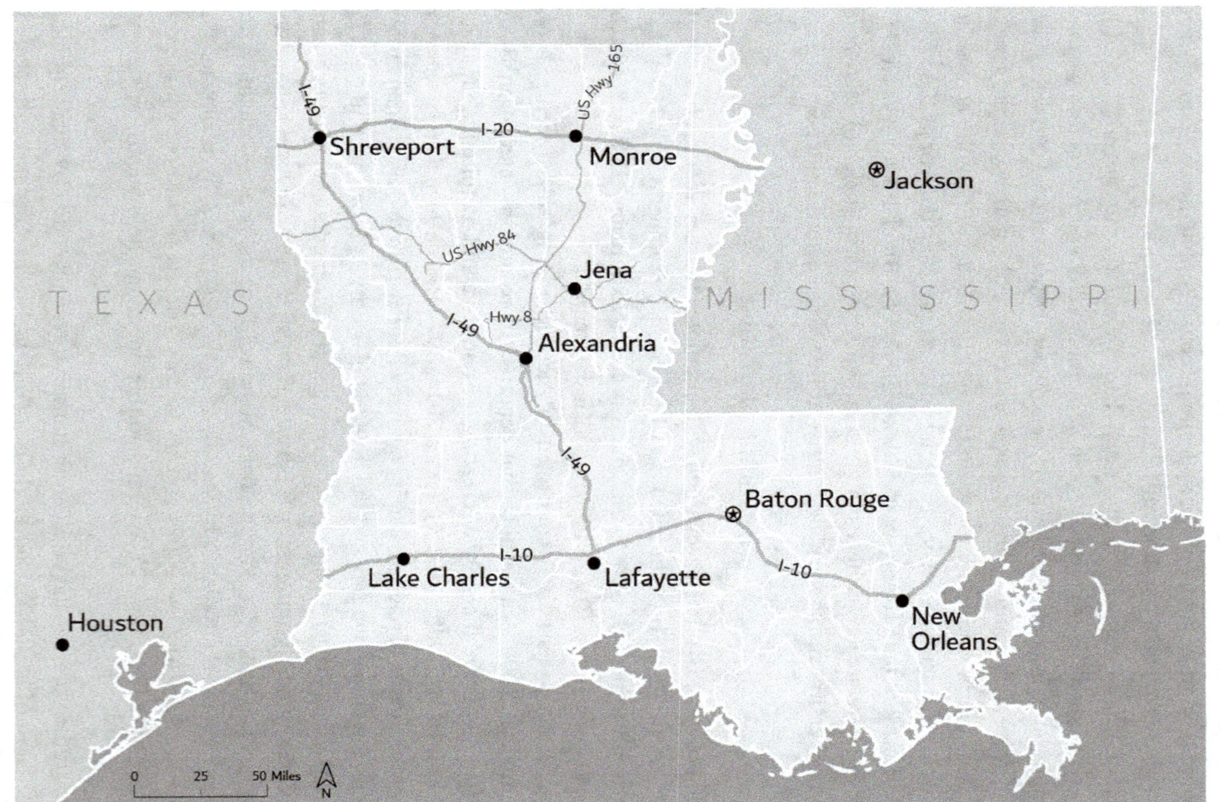

Figure 2 Map of Louisiana showing location of Jena in relation to parish outlines, highways, and larger cities. Map by Anya Shaw.

Jordan Flaherty, whose first story was posted on May 9 to multiple online progressive media outlets. Bean also recruited coverage for a segment on Paula Zahn's CNN show that aired on the eve of Mychal Bell's trial, a month after the other news stories broke.

The May news stories all portrayed Jena as a racist Southern town. Flaherty emphasized persistent local protests and other recent cases of racial violence in nearby towns. Witt and Mangold described Jena as a throwback to Jim Crow era segregation although they also included "both sides" interviews with White residents who described racial harmony. In a blog commenting on the Witt and Mangold stories the day after they were published, Bean said "The Jena story suggests that certain pockets of Deep South American didn't get the civil rights memo. That is certainly the burden of the Jena stories published yesterday." Bean continued: "Jena is being covered as a story about the persistence of the old Jim Crow, but it is much more than that. Jena is also a story about the new Jim Crow: the manipulation of the criminal justice system to deprive low status black people of basic justice" (FOJ 05–21).[6] The "old Jim Crow throwback" framing dominated the circulating narratives.

As the protest campaign unfolded, some writers interviewed the people involved and published divergent claims about the personal relationships and conflicts among the youths involved in the various events, the youths' personal histories and characters, the extent of the punishment the noose-hangers, and the details of the several fights that are part of the story (e.g., Barr and Noren 2007; Christie 2008; Waldman 2008; Franklin 2007). We cannot adjudicate disputes about truth of these claims. Instead, we focus on the construction of the narrative. We compare the events described in contemporaneous sources – drawing primarily on accounts in the Alexandria *Town Talk* and Alan Bean's narrative[7] – with what was said later by media and movement actors. Except as noted, the *Town Talk* and Bean's narrative agree with each other. Our discussion of the narrative as it circulated later is based primarily on sixty-nine Black newspaper articles and thirty-five mainstream newswire articles drawn from our larger research project.[8]

Although the circulating narratives often compressed the timeline, the original time frame has two acts. Act 1 is events between August 31 and September 18 about the noose-hanging. Act 2 is events between November 30 and late December related to the fight. We have no contemporaneous records of what happened in the intervening ten weeks. The narrative task was to connect these seemingly unconnected sets of events. We first discuss the

---

[6] References with FOJ refer to the list of Friends of Justice blog posts in the sources listed in Appendix B.

[7] See Appendix B for citations to sources.   [8] See Appendix C for more details.

narratives constructed about of each of the two acts and then consider what was said about the connections between them.

Act 1: September 2006

The anchor events in the narrative about September were that nooses were hung on a tree at Jena High School after a Black student challenged the assumption that only Whites could sit under it and that the noose-hangers were not seriously punished. A Black student (later identified as Kenneth Purvis, a cousin of Bryant Purvis, one of the Jena 6) asked about sitting under the "white" tree at a school assembly on Thursday August 31. Two hangman's nooses[9] in the school colors were hung on the tree on Friday September 1. The three perpetrators were quickly identified,[10] and the principal recommended expulsion for them on Wednesday September 6. The school board rejected expulsion and instead suspended the students on Thursday September 7. At the time, the school superintendent declined to give further details about the punishment except to say that the students were currently in an alternative school. Bean described the punishment as "a few days suspension" which was later generally rendered as "three days." A year later, at the height of the protest, officials described more extensive punishment including three weeks of several types of suspension, a discipline court, and intervention programs (Christie 2008), but this was not reported at the time.

It is likely that Purvis's original question had a jocular tone and was met by laughter, and possible that the youths who hung the nooses saw it as a prank, but this does not mean the question and the nooses were innocent of racial conflict. What we know for sure is that Black adults in Jena did not view the nooses as an innocent joke. The nooses were hung on Friday before the Labor Day weekend. On Tuesday September 5, Black adults called regional news outlets, including both the Alexandria *Town Talk* and Alexandria television station KALB, and held a protest meeting at L&A Missionary Baptist Church. The story was circulated by the Associated Press and reprinted nationally and internationally.

The *Town Talk* article says that about sixteen students were present at the meeting and stood up to confirm that they had seen the nooses but did not speak. With one exception, the adults quoted in the story did not appear in later stories about the Jena 6. They include Tracy Bowens (who organized the meeting and was later quoted in Howard Witt's May 20 story), Dan Brown (who called reporters), Renea Ogletree (who has contacted the "National Association for the

---

[9] The original *Town Talk* report says two nooses, Alan Bean's narrative and later reports say three nooses.

[10] Their names were never made public because they were juveniles.

Advancement of Colored People's national action network about the incident")[11], Shirley Bowers, and lawyer Krystal Todd (identifiable in other news stories as a public defender). Associated Press articles named Tracy Bowens as having organized a community meeting and printed follow up stories about the recommended expulsion and then lesser punishment of the students. Alexandria television station KALB covered the protest about the nooses initially and in follow up stories.

News coverage of the adult protest on September 5 had consequences the next day. The *Town Talk* reports that there was continuing racial tension on September 6 about the nooses, including at least one fight at school and as many as five fights. Bean's narrative says students conducted an ad hoc protest under the tree that day; the *Town Talk* makes no mention of a protest. Both say a school assembly was called with police present, and the district attorney spoke to the assembly. The *Town Talk* describes the school assembly as a response to the tensions and fights at school in the wake of the noose incident and says that district attorney Reed Walters "stressed the importance of remaining calm." Walters later admitted under oath that he said what Alan Bean's narrative quotes him as saying at the assembly: "I can take away your lives with a stroke of this pen." Black students said that Walters was looking at them when he said it, while Walters claimed he was speaking to all students and addressing the fights that had occurred. In Bean's narrative, Walters's statement is implicitly a threatening response to the protest at school.

In the same articles that describe the ongoing conflict over the nooses and the proposed expulsion and reduced penalty to suspension only of the students who hung the nooses, the *Town Talk* reports that there were fights or threats at school and police patrolled the school on Thursday and Friday, September 7 and 8. The fights at school on these specific dates were not covered by the Associated Press or later articles, although many later articles vaguely referred to "ongoing fights" as if they had persisted throughout the fall.

Black adults persisted in their protests. On September 11, a group asked for but was refused the opportunity to speak to the school board and were quoted as saying they had contacted the NAACP and the FBI. The FBI did, in fact, come to town to investigate, but this was not reported at the time. On September 18, Tracy Bowens was allowed to speak for five minutes to the school board. The *Town Talk* coverage on September 19 says:

> The anger over the nooses incident at Jena High School hasn't died down, yet. Parent Tracy Bowens addressed the LaSalle Parish School Board during its 6

---

[11] The National Association for the Advancement of Colored People and the National Action Network are two separate organizations.

p.m. meeting and said the three students who took part in putting nooses on a tree on the school campus should have been expelled. The students were suspended. "If the proper procedures had been taken, none of this would be going on now," Bowens told the board in a 5-minute speech. "We only want what's right. We want our young people to really be equal and not have to be reminded of the wrong things that were done to our race in the past." Some black parents have said the nooses had racial overtones because they were placed after some black students asked about sitting under a tree as white students do. Bowens, who helped organize a recent meeting at L&A Missionary Baptist Church concerning the incident, told the board that all students should be treated equally. She also indicated that she and other parents will come back before the board on the issue. "We're not just focusing on the three young men. It's for whoever, because right is right. No matter what color you are, something needs to be done to let it be known this will not be allowed from anyone," Bowens said. The board took no action after hearing Bowens speak.

Black adult efforts to attract media attention and address the situation were treated as divisive. On September 13, the *Jena Times* published an editorial blaming the fights at school on media coverage about the nooses.[12] The January 2007 *Jena Times* year in review summarizes this story:

> September 13: Despite a constant barrage of negative media coverage last week concerning Jena High School, officials note that most of the "racial tensions" were more media hype than reality. Jena and Jena High School were featured on numerous television and daily newspaper segments, often claiming the top story location or front page, citing racial tensions from an incident that occurred August 31 at the school.

There was intense community conflict about how to view the intentions of the noose-hangers and the seriousness of the offense. Claims that the nooses were an innocent prank without racial animus were rejected by those who argued that everyone knew or should know the meaning of nooses, especially in the context of it being a response to the previous day's question. Ten months later in a July 26, 2007, forum at Good Pines Middle School attended by more than a hundred mostly Black people, federal officials outlined the definition of a hate crime, and an FBI agent said the noose-hanging met two of the elements of a federal hate crime (motivated by bias, interfered with a protected activity) but not the third, threat or use of force. Then the same official said that expulsion is a common remedy in response to such incidents and noted that as far as they knew, no school official or anyone in political leadership had ever denounced the noose-hanging. Other later discussions emphasize that the nooses met the

---

[12] Although we do not have access to the 2006 copies of the *Jena Times*, both Alan Bean's narrative and comments in letters to the editor in the Town Talk imply this claim.

definition of a hate crime in Louisiana state law and emphasize the failure of the school administration to take the incident seriously and address the concerns of Black residents.

As the Jena campaign built, the circulating narratives gave all the agency of resistance to the nooses to students, not adults. Black students stood silently on September 5 at L&A Baptist Church, while adults spoke and protested. But the circulating narratives erased the documented adult protests while adding less well-documented student protests.

School officials denied knowing about any student protest, and a representative of the FBI reported at the July forum that he could find no evidence that a protest had occurred. It is plausible that some sort of small ad hoc protest took place when Bean says it did on September 6 and that it was linked to the fights reported in the *Town Talk*. YouTube videos posted in the summer and fall of 2007 include Black students describing protests occurring in a variety of ways and on different occasions. Published articles have a wide variety of protest embellishments and some published variants have the students sitting in protest under the tree two or even three times, both before and after the nooses were hung.

Of the early outside reporting on the case, Flaherty mentions a school protest linked to the district attorney's threat at the assembly and the June CNN Paula Zahn show says that students sat under the tree before the nooses, while Witt and Mangold make no mention of student protests. None of early stories nor any of the articles in our project sample mentioned any of the documented adult protests. By contrast, 56% of Black newspaper articles versus 9% of newswire articles mentioned a student protest at the tree after the nooses were hung.[13] Sitting under the tree in protest before the nooses were hung (often substituting for the student asking about sitting under the tree) was described in 56% of Black newspaper articles and 27% of newswire articles. In an August 1 Democracy Now interview, Jordan Flaherty describes the protest even more vividly and implausibly: "And the next day the three nooses were hung from the tree. And in a spontaneous act of daring and brave resistance, nearly every Black student in the school went and stood under the tree" (Goodman 2007).

Act 2: December 2006

Act 2 begins with arson. In the early hours of Thursday November 30, a fire that was obviously arson destroyed the main building of Jena High School. The event was traumatic for the community and was a major topic of multiple local news stories and a brief Associated Press story. Nobody knew who had done it.

---

[13] See Appendix C.

(A year later, a mixed-race group of students unrelated to the Jena 6 incident were charged with the crime.) Black and White students blamed each other. Jena High was closed Thursday and Friday. There were multiple interracial fights that weekend that did not involve the teens later singled out. Teachers asked school officials to delay reopening because of weekend fighting but school reopened Monday anyway.

Jena High School leadership was in transition. In November, the school board voted to transfer Scott Windham, the Jena High principal who had recommend expulsion for the noose-hangers, to supervising maintenance and transportation effective December 1 and to search for a replacement. A new principal was approved at a School Board meeting on December 4 "effective today." This transition and its possible implications about ongoing adult conflicts about the noose incident or its effects on decisions about reopening school were never mentioned in any later article.

After the December 4 fight, two fights on December 1 and 2 became part of the later Jena 6 story. Because the December 1 and 2 fights were brought into the narrative only after the December 4 fight, we discuss the December 4 fight first.

The December 4 Fight and Beating of Justin Barker

Monday December 4 was the first day students were back at school. Classes were operating in makeshift facilities. Shortly after noon, Justin Barker, a White student, was knocked unconscious and beaten by several Black students. The first *Town Talk* news report on December 5 said a student was "beaten pretty badly" and was briefly hospitalized and released the same day. A *Jena Times* story published December 13 gives the tenor of its coverage: "one of the most violent attacks in Jena High School's history did occur by six black students on a lone white student. . . . At the end of the lunch period, the six students jumped a white male student, beating him unconscious with him having to be carried from the school by ambulance to the emergency room. Although he was released later that day it was reported that he has since had to undergo an MRI."

Barker attended an awards ceremony that evening, which was interpreted by many as evidence that he was not seriously harmed. Mangold describes Barker as "his usual smiling self." Witt says Barker was knocked unconscious, but the injuries were "not serious." Barker later said he attended the ceremony because it was important to him but left early because he was in pain. In a June interview for the Paula Zahn show, Barker's mother said she thought there was attempted murder and described the injuries as "Several lacerations on both sides. Both the ears was kind of really damaged, and both eyes. His right eye was the worst. It had blood clots in it." Those close to the case generally acknowledged that Barker had been seriously hurt, even as his injuries were not life-threatening.

There were about forty witnesses including both students and teachers, who gave conflicting accounts of what had happened, who had hit Barker, who had said what, and who was even present and involved in the fight. One teacher witness identified someone who was not charged at all as the first person who hit Barker. Different news stories offered different renditions of the fight details. The official account (as in the *Jena Times* story) was that the Jena 6 had without provocation lain in wait for Barker, knocked him to the ground, and had all kicked him until another student intervened. Other accounts suggested more multilateral fighting. Journalists who read the transcripts of witness statements say that Justin Barker had been following Black students around using racial slurs and taunting them about Robert Bailey having been beaten the previous weekend. The only guilty plea ever entered was Mychal Bell's admission that he had knocked Barker to the floor. The other five pled "no contest" in 2009.

The December 1 and 2 Fights

Although multiple interracial fights occurred over the weekend, officials singled out the December 1 and 2 fights involving Robert Bailey to construct a narrative justifying charging conspiracy to commit murder. Defenders of the Jena 6 construed these two fights as evidence of extreme racial bias by the authorities. For both fights there is agreement about key facts and disagreement about contexts and details.

Successive *Town Talk* articles reveal the construction of the official narrative. A December 6 article reports the arrest of football star Carwin Jones, Robert Bailey, Theo Shaw, and a juvenile for the December 4 fight and says it "may be linked" to a fight on December 2 also involving Shaw and Bailey in which a gun was taken from "the victim" Matt Windham, who was taken to a hospital, treated, and released. A December 7 article says a third fight "also involving Robert Bailey" occurred on December 1 at a private party and that authorities "suspect the fight at the party led to the other two."

On Friday December 1, Robert Bailey was beaten by multiple White males after attempting to enter a party at the Fair Barn where attendees were predominantly White. All accounts agree that the first punch was thrown by a White man, but official reports in the *Town Talk* described Bailey as "involved" in the incident, not as its victim. Accounts differ as to how many people beat him and how badly he was beaten, with Bean's narrative and other accounts saying multiple people punched and kicked him and hit him with a beer bottle, while *Jena Times* editor Craig Franklin's "Truth about Jena" article (Franklin 2007) denies the severity of the attack. The Town Talk says Justin Sloan (age 22) was arrested and charged with misdemeanor battery in the case, implying the arrest occurred on December 6; Bean's narrative says he could find no record of the charge. Bean emphasizes that this fight was a mirror image of the December 4 fight, with multiple people attacking one person, but the charging was very different in the two circumstances, misdemeanor battery in one case and attempted murder in the other.

The competing accounts of the December 2 fight at the Gotta Go market are even more convoluted. All accounts agree that Matt Windham (a White young adult) pulled a shotgun on a group of Black teens who successfully wrested the gun away from him and that Robert Bailey, Theo Shaw, and Ryan Simmons were charged with theft, felony robbery, and disorderly conduct. Bean says that Windham had been involved in the fight the night before. Black accounts generally describe the encounter as beginning when Windham pulled the gun and express outrage at people being charged with stealing the gun when they took it away to defend themselves. Sara Atchison-Brame, then CNN field producer working the Jena story, interviewed the person working at the market that night who said that Windham went to get the gun when he saw the group of Black youths; she also said that the Black youths took the gun to the police within an hour of the incident.[14] The official account is that the Black youths were chasing Windham, who is described as a "victim," and that he retrieved his gun in self-defense. These official accounts do not explain why pulling the gun was an acceptable response or why it was a felony to end the encounter by taking the gun away and leaving with it.

The Charges

The six arrested boys were initially charged with felony second degree battery. The charges for the four who were seventeen or older – Robert Bailey, Theo Shaw, Carwin Jones, and Bryant Purvis – were upgraded to attempted murder on Thursday December 8 with bails set between $70,000 and $138,000. The names of the juveniles were not released. A week later, on December 15, Mychal Bell, age 16, was moved into the adult system with bail set at $90,000. He could only be charged as an adult because of the attempted murder charge; he would have been tried as a juvenile for battery. The sixth student, later identified as Jesse Beard, was fourteen and remained generally unnamed and in the juvenile system. Much later it was reported that there was a seventh student also charged in the case who was a juvenile and was never publicly named. The families of Bryant Purvis, Carwin Jones, and Jesse Beard were able

---

[14] Author interview with Sara Atchison-Brame who said the worker was unwilling to go on record.

to post bond in December so they could get out of jail. The other three, Robert Bailey Jr, Theo Shaw, and Mychal Bell, remained in adult jail because their families could not afford bail.[15] In January, all six were expelled from Jena schools.

The escalated charges to attempted murder appear to be politically motivated by demands in the community to control what was seen as Black-initiated racial violence. In covering the charge upgrade, the *Town Talk* says: "This comes after reports that some teachers were considering a sickout because of discipline problems at the school." A partially redacted article in the *Jena Times* on December 13 also says teachers threatened a sickout on the evening of December 4.

On December 13, District Attorney Reed Walters published an editorial in the *Jena Times* in which he implied that the arrested students were also responsible for the arson and said, "I will not tolerate this type of behavior. To those who act in this manner I tell you that you will be prosecuted to the fullest extent of the law and with the harshest crimes that the facts justify. When you are convicted I will seek the maximum penalty allowed by law. I will see to it that you never again menace the students at any school in this parish."

Nine months later, shortly before the big rally in September 2007, it was publicly revealed that Mychal Bell had previously been convicted of assaults as a juvenile. Several reporters who investigated the case believed that Walters was especially focused on convicting Bell, although the fights deemed relevant to the case centered on Bailey. The three boys who were bailed out in December were arrested later for other assaultive offenses: Jesse Beard in 2007 and Carwin Jones and Bryant Purvis in 2008. Multiple revisionist accounts claim that the accused boys had been preying on the community, but, except for Mychal Bell, and the two incidents discussed above, we have seen no specific claims about violent incidents involving these boys before December 2006.

Community Response

Local news stories imply a widespread belief in the community that racial fighting was a serious community issue that was linked to burning the school. There were reports that students were afraid to go to school. A ministerial association held community healing events led by Black and White Christian ministers that included a December 13 unity prayer service and listening session

---

[15] The families would have to either (a) post the full amount as cash bail, which would be refunded if the person returns to court, or (b) pay a non-refundable 12% of the full amount to have a bail bond company post bail, or (c) put up property such as a home as bond to ensure the defendant's return to court, which would be lost if the defendant did not return.

held at the Jena High School football stadium and prayer walks involving more than 300 people in the four Jena schools. The *Jena Times* devoted multiple pages to these unity events on December 13 and December 20, including several pictures of interracial groups praying. On December 15, White Baptist Minister Eddie Thompson (a member of the ministerial association) posted a blog that describes the unity service, says that the town is "awash in racism," references racial fights all over town, White boys hanging nooses and Black boys attacking pizza delivery trucks, and calls for religious healing (Thompson 2006). The ministerial association held a closed-door session on Thursday December 21 to plan next steps, emphasizing they wanted to involve all faiths and ethnicities and be a positive force, and they asked permission to be present at schools when they reopened.

Overall, Act 2 involves a racial fight that occurred in a context of wider racial fighting in the wake of the school arson and evidence that many in the community saw racial conflict to be a problem that had escalated to violence. Despite its central importance to the community and its having been covered by the Associated Press, the arson was mentioned in only 18% of newswire and 17% of Black newspaper articles about the Jena 6 published through September 20. When the arson was mentioned, it was typically in a list of "escalating tensions" on a par with fights, rather than as a key source of community trauma. The December 1 and 2 fights were mentioned more often than the arson, especially in Black newspapers that highlighted racial bias in responses to those fights. The teachers' sickout threats and the religious racial unity events were never mentioned.

Connecting the Acts and Constructing a Narrative

The power of the Jena 6 narrative was the link between the nooses and the fight. The narrative problem was to explain the connection between events in September and events in December. The authorities repeatedly asserted there was no connection. None of the *Town Talk* stories focusing on the arson mentioned the noose-hanging incident, nor were the nooses mentioned in the first report of the crucial December 4 fight. However, subsequent *Town Talk* articles about the December 4 fight that linked it to fights on December 1 and 2 always contained the official statement that the fights were not related to either the nooses or the arson, a repetition of nonrelevance that implies the possible connection was in public consciousness.

Bean's list of events left the content and character of the connections between September and December ambiguous, saying: "Although few major disciplinary issues emerged during the fall semester at Jena High School, there is strong evidence that several black male students remained unusually agitated through-out the semester and that disciplinary referrals on these students spiked sharply."

Those who dug into the case sometimes suggested that there were ongoing conflicts between a specific group of White boys associated with the rodeo program who included the noose-hangers and a specific group of Black boys associated with the football program who included some of the Jena 6 and that some of the conflicts were personal (including a prior conflict between Justin Barker and Mychal Bell around Barker's girlfriend), but personalized explan-ations were never part of any of the circulating accounts.

One common narrative device for connecting the nooses and the fight in the news articles we examined (including in the three May breakout articles) was "persistent conflict," implying that there had been relatively continuous or at least periodic fighting between September and December (which Alan Bean's spring 2007 narrative explicitly denies). In some cases, the timeline was simply compressed to imply (or even say) that the noose-hanging happened shortly before the crucial fight. A few writers even included Justin Barker being arrested for bringing a gun to school on May 10, 2007, as having occurred at the time of the other fights.

In some variants of the narrative, the connection was simply that the same community was a racist place that had both tolerated noose-hanging and over-charged the youths. In this account, the nooses do not need to explain or have any direct connection to the fight; they are enough as a symbol of how racist Jena is. Greenlea's content analysis of comments on the ColorOfChange.org petition about the Jena 6 finds that by far the most common reference was to the nooses, with 54% mentioning them (Greenlea 2014, 56). Follow-up protests by Black organizations in October and November focused on increasing the penalties for hate crimes, especially noose-hangings. The three breakout stories in May all invoked a "racist place" narrative, with Mangold and Witt empha-sizing throwbacks to Jim Crow and Flaherty emphasizing present-day cases of racist violence in nearby communities. As the conflict unfolded, White Jena residents expressed resentment at being characterized as exceptionally back-ward and racist.

The movement problem with the "racist place" narrative is that it localizes the problem to Jena only. Both Alan Bean and Black movement leaders repeatedly sought to generalize, tying the Jena case to broader national problems of unequal treatment, treating Jena not as an unusual throwback but as symptom-atic of current problems in the whole country, what Bean often called the "new Jim Crow."

For many circulating the story, there was a narrative storytelling drive to forge a more direct connection between the nooses and the fight, making the nooses a cause of the fight and the fight an act of resistance against racial intimidation. Some said that the failure to punish the noose-hanging encouraged more racial taunting by White students against Black students. Perhaps this is what people were euphemistically referring to as "racial tensions" and what Bean is referring to in this July 10 blog post:

> When you hang a noose, you say: "we white people are going to torture you black people to death if you don't stay in your place." This was a fight provoked by a hate crime. After the school refused to punish this hate crime and take a stand for racial equality, the grownups left the white and black kids to fight it on their own. Then only the black kids were punished for the fight that took place as a result, while the white kids were coddled as innocent victims.

Bean's statement makes the fighting sound like an apolitical defensive reaction to the hate crime. Other versions of the connection turned the fight more into an act of resistance against racism. Some accounts emphasized that Barker was friends with one of the students who had hung the nooses. Accounts stressing that Justin Barker was heard racially taunting Black students before the fight implicitly invoked the idea of "fighting words" and fighting as resistance to racism. Some accounts even claimed that the reason for the overcharging was that the Jena 6 themselves had organized a student protest about the nooses. For example, in the previously cited Democracy Now interview, Jordan Flaherty followed the description of the school protest with: "And it's been widely said that the folks that organized that protest to sit under the tree are the so-called Jena Six, the six students that are now facing life in prison for a schoolyard fight" (Goodman 2007).

Adult Conflict and Collective Action

The Jena 6 narrative as it circulated typically treated these six Black students as standing alone or only with other students in resisting the racial oppression of the nooses, first in conducting a protest at an uncertain time that seemed to expand in importance with the telling and then in the fight itself, which was described as resistance to racial taunting and sometimes even as specifically about the nooses. This narrative impulse aligns with Polletta's arguments about how openness and spontaneity can help recruit participants to action. In these narratives, the Jena 6 themselves were the only significant actors. The District Attorney's overcharging was motivated either by static racism or as retribution for student protest about the nooses.

These variants of the Jena 6 narrative erased the adult collective action in September that included holding a protest meeting, obtaining outside media coverage, protesting at the school board, and bringing the FBI to town. They erased White adult hostility toward the outside media attention. They erased the community trauma of the school arson. They erased evidence of broader adult political pressure to bring violence under control that included the teachers' threatened sick-in. They erased evidence of widespread community concern about racial conflict in the adult-led biracial community-wide religious racial healing events.

An alternate narrative locates the over-charging of the Jena 6 in the context of wider community racial conflict and the perception that this racial conflict had become violent. This is the emphasis in the email circulated via the Juvenile Justice Project: "The circumstances surrounding these arrests paint a disturbing picture of a community mired in racial tension. . ." (quoted in Flaherty 2010, 340). The authorities blamed arson and racial fighting only on Black students and sought to bring the situation under control with excessive punitiveness toward the arrested Black youths.

The *Jena Times* had said that the noose incident was a prank that had been overblown and blamed news coverage for creating conflict. A *Jena Times* article dated January 10, 2007, says: "As the year 2006 ended, Jena High School and the community witness tensions resulting in a fire that destroyed the main educational building at the school and student fights on and off campus, which resulted in several arrests." This sentence structure says that "tensions" preceded and caused both the fire and fights. In context, "tensions" seems to refer to conflicts around the noose incident.

While we cannot assess the distribution of community opinions about the Jena 6 from this distance, the community racial unity events demonstrate that many people of both races saw a community-wide problem that went beyond that one fight and called for a more bilateral need for healing and reconciliation. Even as they differed from the punitive response, these racial unity events were not necessarily addressing racial injustice. Greenlea (2014, 34) critiques the unity rallies as requiring Black people to set aside their complaints and return to the status quo and says that the families insisted instead on organizing resistance. Bean says, "the price of unity was steep—no one, black or white, was allowed to reference the plight of the Jena 6, the 'noose incident' or any other real-world event. As a result, the six young men accused of attempted murder were left to twist in the wind" (FOJ 08–18). Bean continues to say that only Antioch Baptist would allow meetings about the case, and that Black people supported the case privately but not publicly because "That would mean getting the white folks upset, and, Lord knows, we don't want that." Emerson and Smith

(2001) discuss the national-level attempts at racial reconciliation among Evangelicals in the 1990s, arguing that these movements ultimately failed because White Evangelicals saw this happening entirely at the level of individual personal relationships, while Black Evangelicals believed that issues of systemic racism also needed to be addressed. Jena's interracial ministerial association fell apart as the case progressed in 2007.

3 Mobilizing Support

This section provides a process tracing of how the Jena 6 campaign built over time. It begins by locating the case in its historical context and then provides details about the three phases of the mobilization: the local and regional efforts between January and June; the involvement of national organizations in July and August after Mychal Bell's guilty verdict at the end of June; and the communications and mobilizing cascade that began after the mid-August call for a protest in September. News sources supporting the process tracing are provided in Appendix B. Overall, the first two phases involved ordinary mobilizing around the case that was initially unsuccessful but then became successful in gaining support for the Jena 6. The third phase shifted emphasis from the case itself to a movement-building attempt that kicked off a cascade of communication and collective action.

Historical Context

Historians use the term "Long Civil Rights Movement" to describe the decades of organizing and protest that preceded the conventionally defined Civil Rights Era (Burke 2020; Cha-Jua and Lang 2007; Felber 2020; Fujino and Harmachis 2020; Kelley 2010; Morris 1984; Nichter 2014, 2021; Stillerman 2020; Williams 2015). What may be called the Long Black Movement continued from the end of the Civil Rights era into the rise of the Black Lives movement in 2014. Rollbacks of Civil Rights gains began in the 1970s (Robnett 2020) and ensuing decades saw both gains and losses. Although weakened, NAACP, SCLC, CORE, and hundreds of other national and local organizations continued to promote Black interests in a wide variety of ways with a wide range of political ideologies (Brewer 2003; Johnson 2007; Lawson 2014; Marable 2007; Musgrove 2019; Oliver 2020; Richie 2012; Taylor 2015).

The 1990s saw Black disenchantment after the not guilty verdict for the police who beat Rodney King in 1992 and the Republican victories of 1994. Organizing for the 1995 Million Man March built support and raised civic and political participation across a wide range of Black demographics and political ideologies, despite controversies around Louis Farrakhan and the Nation of

Islam, but there was widespread disappointment that no national-level organization emerged from it (Rahman 1996).

Cathy Cohen (2010, 170) calls hurricane Katrina the "Rodney King moment" for young Black people in the 2000s. In late August 2005, Katrina killed 1,392 people, caused extensive damage on the gulf coast, and displaced about 600,000 households for more than a month. New Orleans flooding disproportionately affected its Black residents and over half of New Orleans's residents were still displaced a year later. Black people identified with hurricane victims and saw racism playing a huge role in the failed disaster response (Harris-Perry 2011, Chapter 4). Displaced activists and writers from New Orleans formed networks to address the ongoing needs and grievances of gulf coast residents (Flaherty 2010)[16] and became one of the channels of organizing for the Jena 6.

The October 12, 2005, Millions More Movement rally organized by Louis Farrakhan and the Nation of Islam commemorated the 10th anniversary of the Million Man March. It was endorsed without controversy by virtually every Black organization. Its stated intention was to build a Black agenda and a sustained movement organization. A few hundred thousand people attended. Rally speeches criticized the failed emergency response to Katrina, criticized the war in Iraq, and emphasized the broad ideological diversity of those in attendance.

The huge pro-immigrant marches in 2006 were generally supported by Black organizations, but some Black newspaper editorialists drew comparisons that decried the absence of comparable attention to Black concerns (e.g., Chicago Citizen 2006; Recorder 2006). Barack Obama, who later became the first Black president, was receiving substantial attention in 2007 as a Democratic candidate.

Phase One, January to May: Regional Support and Media Outreach

Although information about initial local organizing is sparse, its contours can be traced. The six boys accused of attempted murder in Jena received support from activists in the region who were notified through existing activist networks. These initial efforts at ordinary local and regional mobilizing created a local organization, attracted media attention, and produced a barely detectable rise in public attention after mid-June, but these efforts were not enough to obtain help for the Jena 6.

In January 2007, all six boys had been expelled from Jena schools. Robert Bailey, Theo Shaw, and Mychal Bell were sitting in adult jail and already being

---

[16] This point was also stressed by Lamar White in an interview.

punished because their families could not afford to post bail. The families of the other three boys had bailed them out and arranged for them to go elsewhere for schooling while they awaited trial. Black and White ministers sought to calm down tensions as classes resumed at Jena High School.

Regional activists were notified within days of the attempted murder charge through emails circulated through the Juvenile Justice Project of Louisiana (JJPL), a group based in New Orleans that had previously organized against the juvenile prison in Jena (Greenlea 2014, 27). Writer-activist Jordan Flaherty cites the email he received in early December from Jason Williamson, an attorney with JJPL Other evidence of immediate regional awareness is a December 12 blog post titled "Open Thread: What the Heck Is Happening in Jena?" (White 2006) by Lamar White, then an aide to the newly elected mayor of Alexandria:

> It seems like our neighbors up in Jena are having a difficult time with their teenagers (and with racism). Back in September, a group of white students were suspended (not expelled, as many parents had hoped) for putting a pair of hangman's nooses in a tree on the campus of Jena High School. Then, someone burns the school down. And now, four kids are being charged with attempted second degree murder in a bizarre story involving a stolen gun.

Three comments dated December 12 to 14 offer garbled versions of the Gotta Go fight, complain that the *Town Talk* isn't investigating, discuss the story about the gun, and say, "LaSalle Parish is well known as a Klan area." The fourth and final comment dated January 24 is from Alan Bean, saying he plans to come to town soon and would like to talk to anyone who knows anything, giving his phone number. Bean left a similar undated comment on Eddie Thompson's December 15 "awash with racism" post, mentioned above.

Local and Regional Media

We have access to archives of the Alexandria *Town Talk* and the *Jena Times* for 2007, but not for radio or television outlets. Alexandria radio host Tony Brown's Eyes Wide Open show covered the Jena story from the beginning (FOJ 09–10) and Brown claimed to have been the first to use the "Jena 6" tag (DeRienzo 2007). The *Jena Times* covered the unfolding court cases and provided detailed coverage of protests in Jena that involved outsiders. The Alexandria *Town Talk*, which had covered the noose incident in the fall and the arson and fight in December, published a few articles covering the developing court cases and then began covering the protest movement regularly after May 2. A local public access television station in Lafayette also became involved at some point in the spring (Flaherty 2010). Alexandria television station KALB had covered the noose incident in the fall and later began covering the unfolding protest movement. Other Louisiana media sources picked up the case as it unfolded.

Alan Bean and Friends of Justice

Alan Bean is an ordained Baptist minister who founded a small advocacy group based in Texas called Friends of Justice that focuses on bringing media attention and outside support to cases in rural parts of the South typically overlooked by national organizations and media. Like Flaherty, Bean learned of the Jena case via the Juvenile Justice Project of Louisiana (JJPL). He received an email from Derwyn Bunton, then a federal public defender affiliated with the JJPL and later chief legal officer for the Southern Poverty Law Center. Bunton first constructed the noose-fight narrative and credits Bean for pursuing the case:

> [Bean] wouldn't take no for an answer. And what he also did, he was in a way that others weren't able to – to make folks understand that if this is the sort of oppression and injustice that you think is run-off-the-mill, then shame on you. It made folks really think, god, you're right. And I think folks around these parts had become used to injustice, just being normal. (Goodwyn 2008)[17]

Bean has said in several venues (e.g., Bean 2010) that he was the first person from outside to express interest in the case, that nobody else had an effective strategy for intervening, and that media coverage was necessary to attract outside pro bono legal support. The Friends of Justice website[18] describes the contours of the mobilization with an emphasis on the legal case:

> At the request of affected families in Jena, Friends of Justice director Alan Bean conducted a thorough investigation of the case and created an aggressive justice coalition involving Friends of Justice, the Louisiana branches of the American Civil Liberties Union and the National Association for the Advancement of Colored People. Soon, the case was being covered by media as diverse as the British Broadcasting Corporation and the Chicago Tribune.
>
> Gradually, Friends of Justice was able to bring a diverse coalition of partners to the table including the American Civil Liberties Union, the Southern Poverty Law Center, Color of Change, and the Legal Defense Fund of the NAACP. When leaders and students from schools like Howard University and Harvard University joined the movement it became possible to recruit gifted pro bono attorneys from Louisiana, Mississippi and leading law firms in Chicago and New York City. By the time 30,000 people from across the nation came to Jena to demand equal justice for the Jena 6 the legal fight was in exceptionally good hands. When the crowds returned home the legal fight continued unabated.

---

[17] Derwyn Bunton's surname is misspelled in this transcript.
[18] https://friendsofjustice.blog/completed-campaigns/.

Regional Allies: Louisiana NAACP, ACLU, NAN, and others

The level of involvement of Louisiana NAACP in local organizing is somewhat unclear. Some accounts omit (Flaherty 2010) or downplay (Greenlea 2014, 34–37) its role. After the big protest was over, the NAACP's *Crisis* (Spencer 2007) claimed credit for local organizing, saying that help from Louisiana NAACP had begun when family members connected at the January 2007 state convention and that NAACP representatives met with families biweekly and worked with community organizations on broader issues as well as supporting the Jena 6. No specific NAACP organizer is ever named. Although some accounts credit Alan Bean for local organizing, he told the first author in an interview that he was not involved, although he knew meetings were happening. Bean said that he went with the families to the NAACP state convention, where Louisiana NAACP chair Ernest Johnson told them they needed to form a local NAACP chapter. Bean said that he and others were unhappy with this response and that he thought it was "transactional." This is an example of the difference in emphasis between the legal action network and the Black organizations.

Unhappy or not, Caseptla Bailey and others formed an NAACP chapter. The *Jena Times* reported that a meeting of over 100 people at Antioch Baptist Church had founded a LaSalle Parish chapter of the NAACP on March 7 with Caseptla Bailey as chair. King Downing of the ACLU's Campaign for Racial Profiling spoke at the event. His visit to Jena had been added to a tour of Louisiana cities otherwise sponsored by local ACLU chapters and campus law societies. Tory Pegram from Louisiana ACLU was also there. The "Jena Six Defense Committee" was reported to be planning events as part of this group. The next day, March 8, about forty people held a rally in front of the courthouse. The *Jena Times* quotes Downing:

> "I've come down from New York and will keep coming back until justice is served," he said "If we have to bring the cameras of the world here to get justice . . . then we will. We've done that in the past." Downing then led the group in cheers directed toward the courthouse, shouting, "No justice – no peace."

When the national NAACP endorsed the Jena 6 case in its July annual meeting, it specifically referenced the chartering of a LaSalle Parish NAACP chapter in May 2007 as a reason to endorse. The Louisiana NAACP also claimed credit for organizing a July forum about the case attended by over a hundred local Black residents. Although more than a hundred people were reported as joining the NAACP and attending meetings, only Caseptla Bailey is named in news stories about it. She is also reported as speaking to the school board in May on behalf of the NAACP. Later, in October 2007, Rev. Brian Moran, pastor of Antioch

Baptist Church, was identified as the chair of LaSalle Parish NAACP in giving Congressional testimony.

Tory Pegram from Louisiana ACLU visited Jena often after March 8 and became close to Casepta Bailey (Flaherty 2010). Bail bond was posted for Robert Bailey to get out of jail in April, after the ACLU became involved, although we do not know whether that was a factor. Pegram encouraged Jordan Flaherty to attend a rally on May 2, which led to the first nonlocal news story about the case.

The May 2 protest was covered by the *Jena Times*, Abbey Brown of the *Town Talk*, and New Orleans writer-activist Jordan Flaherty. About forty people were present, including King Downing, who spoke promising support from the ACLU and NAACP, and Raymond Brown, leader of the New Orleans chapter of the National Action Network (NAN), Al Sharpton's organization. There were also many plainclothes state troopers present, who were apparently concerned about Raymond Brown's perceived radicalism.[19]

Abbey Brown's article emphasized the young people who were charged and their parents' concerns for them. The *Jena Times* devoted most of its coverage to Raymond Brown's speech, saying he called Jena the most racist place in America and named as racist a wide swath of the community, including Jena First Baptist pastor Dominick DiCarlo, who had organized the interracial ministerial alliance holding community unity meetings. Brown threatened protests, marches, and boycotts by NAN if the charges were not dropped. The *Jena Times* also cited an unnamed source who said Brown went too far and that the families want peace and unity, not radical division.

Launching the Narrative

A 2008 retrospective article about the importance of bloggers says, "Efforts by the Louisiana NAACP and local chapters fell short when a rally they organized last March in support of the Jena 6 teens drew only a few dozen people" (Faison 2008). But this retrospective misses the important point that the March rally happened **because** there was outside support. The article continues: "Though well-intended, their outcome paled in comparison to the whirlwind of support that followed as a result of Internet campaigns." But where did those Internet campaigns come from? The answer is that regional allies crafted a narrative and recruited reporters. The case overview and event list compiled by Derwyn Bunton and Alan Bean from local Black residents and activists became the basis for the later Jena 6 narratives that went viral. Tory Pegram of the ACLU

---

[19] Flaherty (2010) says that when he was visiting Caseptla Brown the day before the rally, state troopers were asking them about Brown, whom they considered a dangerous radical.

recruited Jordan Flaherty to attend the May 2 rally and later recruited law professor Bill Quigley to write an influential July 7 blog post.[20] Alan Bean recruited Tom Mangold of the BBC and Howard Witt of the Chicago Tribune, whose pieces appeared on May 20. Bean also recruited CNN for a segment of the Paula Zahn show that ultimately aired on June 25.

Jordan Flaherty's article (Flaherty 2007a) about the protest is the first non-local coverage of the Jena 6 case. It was published online May 9 on *Left Turn*, a news blog he edited, and was reprinted widely by other progressive and Black media outlets including *Counterpunch*, one of the most popular left-wing outlets. He opens with Alan Bean speaking at the rally organized by local residents, with many state troopers looking on, and attended by allies from other northern and central Louisiana towns, as well as representatives from the ACLU, NAACP, and NAN. He does not mention Raymond Brown. He says: "In the space of a few weeks, more than 150 of this small town's residents have organized an inspiring grassroots struggle against injustice." He devotes extensive attention to Alan Bean and Friends of Justice, citing its mission to focus on small Southern towns that are often neglected by outsiders. His recap of the 2006 events drawing on Bean's narrative includes the protest at the school and the District Attorney's comment as a response to it. Flaherty also discusses the recent murder of a newly elected Black mayor in a nearby town, and shots being fired into the house of another Black mayor in the region. Flaherty tells a story of the local adults exercising agency and having support from regional allies in their struggle. Flaherty went on to write multiple articles for and give multiple interviews to progressive media publicizing the Jena case.

The May 2 rally also provoked local blog commentary (White 2007) which initially received only local comments but began receiving comments from AfroSpear bloggers after May 20.

On May 3, Bean posted on his blog that the White establishment is coming to recognize the prosecutorial overreach and said, "Stay tuned folks–this story will soon be receiving that national coverage it richly deserves" (FOJ 05–03). On May 10 he posted that Jordan Flaherty's story "is being widely circulated by newsletters like Counterpunch" (FOJ 05–10).

Tom Mangold spent three weeks filming in Jena. The blog advertising Mangold's May 24 BBC documentary was posted on the BBC website and published as an article in the online US edition of the *Guardian* on May 20 (Mangold 2007b). The *Guardian* version was widely reprinted in the United States and internationally, including in some Black newspapers (e.g., Mangold 2007a, 2007c). Mangold opens with the upcoming "race trial" and evokes the

---

[20] Personal email communications from Jordan Flaherty and Bill Quigley.

Mississippi Burning Sixties, Selma, and Montgomery, calling Jena an example of the new "stealth" racism and the demons of the Old South. He includes interviews with residents about racial segregation in the community, quotes the provocative statement by district attorney Walters in the local newspaper, and says the NAACP and ACLU "have become involved and have begun to recruit, enthuse, and empower the local black population." It also says, "Jena does not like this publicity and shifts uncomfortably in the glare."

Howard Witt of the *Chicago Tribune* was based in Houston at the time. He spent three days in Jena, reviewed court records, and interviewed two dozen people including as many officials as would talk to him (FOJ 10–02). He quotes Joe Cook, executive director of the Louisiana chapter of the ACLU as calling Jena "a racial powder keg" and Tracy Bowens, referencing her prior protest about the nooses at a school board meeting and says Jena is confronting "old South racial demons." Witt quotes from Eddie Thompson's "awash in racism" blog post (Thompson 2006), cites the series of fights, includes claims that the victim of the fight was friends with the noose-hangers and had been racially taunting the youths, and ends with Justin Barker's May 10 arrest for having a rifle at school.

Bean blogged about these articles on May 21 saying both stories "have entered the Blogosphere," have been reprinted in multiple places, and suggest "that certain pockets of Deep South America didn't get the civil rights memo" (FOJ 05–21). He continues:

> Would this story be attracting so much media attention if it had nothing to offer but an addled DA over-reacting to a school fight – even if the hapless defendants were facing multi-decade sentences without parole? I suspect not. So thank God for the nooses hanging in the school yard! These vile reminders of lynch mob morality have attracted attention to an all-too familiar story that rarely gets much attention.

Reaction in Jena

While it was later claimed that "nobody" in mainstream media paid attention to the Jena 6 case until September, for Jena residents, the Mangold and Witt pieces had already put them in the spotlight by the end of May. An editorial in the *Jena Times* on May 30 complains about the BBC crew who came "two months ago" and "stayed in Jena for some three weeks, filming people in town," received southern hospitality, and in one broadcast transformed the town "from a quaint, quiet little town of wonderful people into a 1960's radical racist hot bed that is out to get everyone of a dark skin color" and that a multi-hour interview with the editor was edited down to make him sound ignorant. Rev. Eddie Thompson, who had posted the "awash with racism" blog in December, complained on

March 22 (Thompson 2007b) about "carpetbaggers" and "visitors with agendas" coming to town and providing "headlines for a controversy-hungry media" and complained on May 23 (Thompson 2007a) that "national media" including the Witt article quoting his blog were distorting the situation in Jena and said: "If the charges of second degree murder against the 'Jena Six' raised the racial tension in Jena, the coverage of the events of the last eight months has ratcheted it up significantly."

Robert Bailey told the *Town Talk* in early June that he had "noticed the national and international attention the case has garnered" and that news coverage had already helped him and the others. The Jena 6 segment of the CNN's Paula Zahn show filmed in late May or early June[21] begins with someone shouting at the reporter who says: "Reporters are not welcome these days at Jena High School where racial tension has led to charges of attempted murder."

June 25–28: Trial and Media Coverage

Mychal Bell and Theo Shaw, who were both still in jail because they could not post $90,000 bond, were scheduled to go to trial on May 21. The trial was postponed over the objections of their attorneys to June 26 at the request of the district attorney who said he did not have his witnesses ready. Some accounts assert that the jury chosen for May 21 was majority Black and say this was the true reason for the DA's postponement request. Robert Bailey, who had been bailed out of jail in April, had also originally been scheduled to go to trial on May 21, but his attorney had requested a postponement.

Only Bell ultimately went to trial on June 26. The attempted murder charges were reduced to felony battery just before the trial began. Bell's court-appointed lawyer wanted him to take a plea bargain and put on no defense. On the eve of the trial June 25, Alan Bean blogged (FOJ 06–25) that media coverage was going to increase, that CNN's Paula Zahn show was covering the trial that evening, that the *Chicago Tribune* would do another story, and another British television station was interested. The trial was covered by the AP's New Orleans-based writer Mary Foster, Howard Witt of the *Chicago Tribune*, and Abbey Brown of the *Town Talk* (whose articles were reprinted in other Louisiana outlets). All three journalists mentioned the all-White jury,[22] only White witnesses, Justin Barker's inability to identify his assailant, the defense

---

[21] It was originally scheduled to air on June 11.

[22] Only Whites were among the 50 people who responded to the jury summons sent to 150 people. There are claims that Black potential jurors had been intimidated along with claims that the jury pool for the original trial date of May 21 was disproportionately Black.

attorney's unwillingness to go to trial or to put on any witnesses favorable to the defense, claims that the charges were excessive, contradictions in witness testimony, and that shoes had been defined as a dangerous weapon to justify the felony charge. All reminded the readers of the September noose incidents, and Witt explicitly invoked a narrative where the nooses were the beginning of the events leading to racial unrest and the fight. Brown and Witt also quoted Alan Bean as saying, "I have never seen a more distressing miscarriage of justice than what happened in LaSalle Parish yesterday." These journalists' reports of what appeared to be an unfair trial led to further attention to the case, but not a media cascade.

Family members were not permitted to be in the courtroom during the trial and were denied the right to protest during the trial (FOJ 06–26). The day after the trial verdict, there was a small protest of about 30 people covered by Abbey Brown of the *Town Talk* but not by outside media. Raymond Brown of NAN was present. The families vowed to continue the fight, and the father of Theo Shaw pled with those present to help him raise the additional money needed to bail his son out of jail. The *Town Talk* story says: "Included on the list of demands [Caseptla] Bailey read during the rally were: that all of the charges be dropped against the students; that the six students receive their credits back from the school; that nothing from the incident be included in juvenile crime records; that an investigation be made into the nooses found hanging at the school in September; and that an investigation be made of Walters and alleged unethical behavior."

Phase Two, July to Early August: Nationalizing the Campaign

Pulled in through existing movement connections, national organizations began supporting the Jena 6 case in July, after Mychal Bell's guilty verdict. Activists organized toward July 31, Bell's scheduled sentencing date. News coverage grew, primarily in Louisiana, progressive, and Black-centric outlets including at least one mention in Tom Joyner's BlackAmericaWeb.com (FOJ 07–02),[23] but also on CNN, NPR, and other mainstream outlets. The *New York Times* was still not covering the case.

The NAACP adopted an emergency resolution about Jena at its national convention held July 7–12, 2007 (NAACP 2007; Spencer 2007). The resolution references the chartering of the LaSalle Parish NAACP in May and its request for "support of the NAACP in demonstrating to the local community that they are not alone in their fight for equal justice for the Jena 6," expresses solidarity,

---

[23] The Internet Archive shows that the story was covered but does not have the text of the story. https://web.archive.org/web/20070701034154/www.blackamericaweb.com/.

and calls on the US Department of justice to investigate and monitor the trial and the US Department of Education to investigate allegations of discrimination in Jena High. Once it took on the issue, the NAACP also opened a web site to collect donations for the Jena 6 (which initially went to general support for the NAACP until there were complaints), issued statements of support, and circulated a petition (Kane 2007).

ColorOfChange.org (COC) is an online organizing hub created by James Rucker, who had previously worked with MoveOn.org. Rucker was from New Orleans but living in San Francisco in 2007. COC's first campaign about racial biases in the treatment of victims of hurricane Katrina gained little response. Rucker heard of the Jena case "from journalists and activists he had worked with on Hurricane Katrina" (Greenlea 2014, 99).[24] Rucker went to Jena to investigate for himself before opening the campaign. The first COC email, sent July 17, began: "The noose-hanging incident and the DA's visit to the school set the stage for everything that followed." By July 31, COC had collected 45,000 signatures on a petition to the Louisiana Governor asking for relief for the Jena 6, which Rucker delivered in person as large stacks of paper at the July 31 protest in Jena. Greenlea says that Rucker helped to organize the July 31 protest.

Although Rucker had previously worked with news media, he decided to work with bloggers in publicizing this case (Greenlea 2014, 181). Comments on AfroSpear blog posts from May and June 2007 that were still extant in 2023 became more frequent in July and August, suggesting that the readership and impact of the blogs accelerated in July, possibly due to the involvement of COC.

The Nation of Islam (NOI) became one of the key pillars of organizing around the Jena case. In 2005, it had formed the Millions More Movement (MMM), which included Christian and secular groups, to advance a more collaborative political agenda. A south Texas member heard about the case from a *Democracy Now* broadcast and texted Jesse Muhammad (now Abdul Qiyam Muhammad) (Greenlea 2014, 125). Muhammad organized a trip to investigate and on July 22 published a cover feature about the Jena 6 for the Nation of Islam's paper, the *Final Call* (Muhammad 2007). The article focuses on the Jena 6 narrative and the unfairness of Bell's trial, quoting Marcus Jones, Mycal Bell's father. It says there will be a protest on July 31 and provides contact information for the MMM to donate funds or support the protest. Muhammad and other members of Houston's NOI called all the organizers of student governments in historically Black colleges and raised grassroots energy

---

[24] Rucker was on Jordan Flaherty's email list that discussed the case. Tory Pegram also communicated with Rucker and probably others did as well (Source: Email communication with Jordan Flaherty).

(Flaherty 2010). The *Final Call* continued to give extensive coverage of the Jena 6 as the mobilization built in August and September (D.-M. Gibson 2012) and the MMM got many people to Jena.

Back in Jena

The ongoing conflict and collective action in Jena were rarely mentioned by outside sources. On July 10, two men were arrested for driving over and destroying the church sign at Antioch Baptist Church, where most of the organizing meetings about the nooses and the Jena 6 were being held. Black residents and Alan Bean called it a hate crime, while the district attorney claimed it was just a prank (FOJ 07–17). On July 26, 161 mostly Black residents attended a forum about the nooses and the Jena 6 case at Good Pine Middle School organized by the NAACP that featured speakers from the FBI and the US attorney (Spencer 2007; Washington Informer 2007).

Mychal Bell was originally scheduled to be sentenced on July 31. On July 31, hundreds of people protested in Jena. Most attendees were from the region, although some were from California, Chicago, and New York. The organizational affiliations of attendees who physically showed up sound like they were primarily recruited through networks of grassroots organizations, not online appeals. The largest groups were Millions More Movement delegations from Houston, Monroe, and Shreveport and nearly fifty members of Families and Friends of Louisiana's Incarcerated Children from Lake Charles and New Orleans (Flaherty 2007b). Other organizations represented included Malcolm X Grassroots Movement, Friends of Justice, Interfaith for Justice, Common Ground of New Orleans, Community Defenders of Lafayette, N'CORBRA, ACLU, INCITE Women of Color Against Violence, Critical Resistance, and Concordia-Catahoula and LaSalle Parishes NAACP.

Jena Times coverage provided the additional information that the reason sentencing had been postponed was the Mychal Bell had fired his prior attorney and now had four attorneys from the region working *pro bono* on his case. Alan Bean's stated objective of drawing in high-powered legal support had been achieved.

The Civil Rights Establishment Arrives

National Civil Rights leaders began arriving in Jena in August. Al Sharpton met with Mychal Bell and his supporters at the courthouse and attended a worship service on August 4. Bell's family asked Sharpton for help in July, and Sharpton had Bell's parents on his radio show three times before he visited Jena (Donica

2007). Sharpton later said he first learned of the case from Raymond Brown of New Orleans NAN. *The Jena Times* devoted a full page to Al Sharpton's visit, including quoting a 1075-word sermon. It devoted much of another page to a complaint that the media had presented a distorted view of the Jena 6, in the process describing frequent media contacts being made to people in Jena. Sharpton's visit was also covered by Mary Foster for the Associated Press. A somewhat different report by her in the *Sacramento Observer* quotes Sharpton as saying he would keep coming back to the town "until justice rains down like water." This phrasing is not in Foster's AP story.

Al Sharpton returned on August 14 along with Martin Luther King III to hold a town hall meeting at Antioch Baptist Church. Jesse Jackson's first trip to Jena was on September 9, when he met with family and attended an event at a local school and was reported as saying he would help lead a march on September 20 that was organized by Rainbow/PUSH.

Other support for the case expanded after the July 31 protest. The Southern Poverty Law Center, the Congressional Black Caucus, the city of Cambridge Massachusetts, and many other groups added their support in August and early September. The NAACP's *Crisis* reported on the supporting organizations who were decrying the charges as gross injustices that do not fit the crime and also said that Charles Ogletree, director of the Charles Hamilton Houston Institute for Race & Justice at Harvard Law School, "has enlisted the help of some of the nation's top criminal justice experts" (Raeshun 2007).

Ordinary Communication and Attention before the Cascade

There was a media cascade about Jena 6 that was mostly centered on the September 20 protest. Figures 3 and 4 summarize more detailed analyses in Appendix E. They show normalized counts of articles (top three panels) and Google searches (bottom panel) for September 1 to October 10 (Figure 3) and May 1 to September 15 (Figure 4). All counts are rescaled as proportions of the maximum within the graphed range, which is set to 100. Figure 3 shows a huge peak in Google searches and mainstream news that is narrowly centered on September 20. Black newspapers tracked by Ethnic NewsWatch had more dispersed coverage in this range.

Earlier patterns that are too small to be detected against the September 20 peak can be seen in Figure 4. The communication and attention cascade started at the end of August. Between May 1 and August 20 there are small bursts of mainstream coverage around the May 20 articles, around Mycal Bell's trial at the end of June, and around the protest on July 31 and Al Sharpton's visit to Jena in early August. Prior to mid-August, most of the coverage archived in US

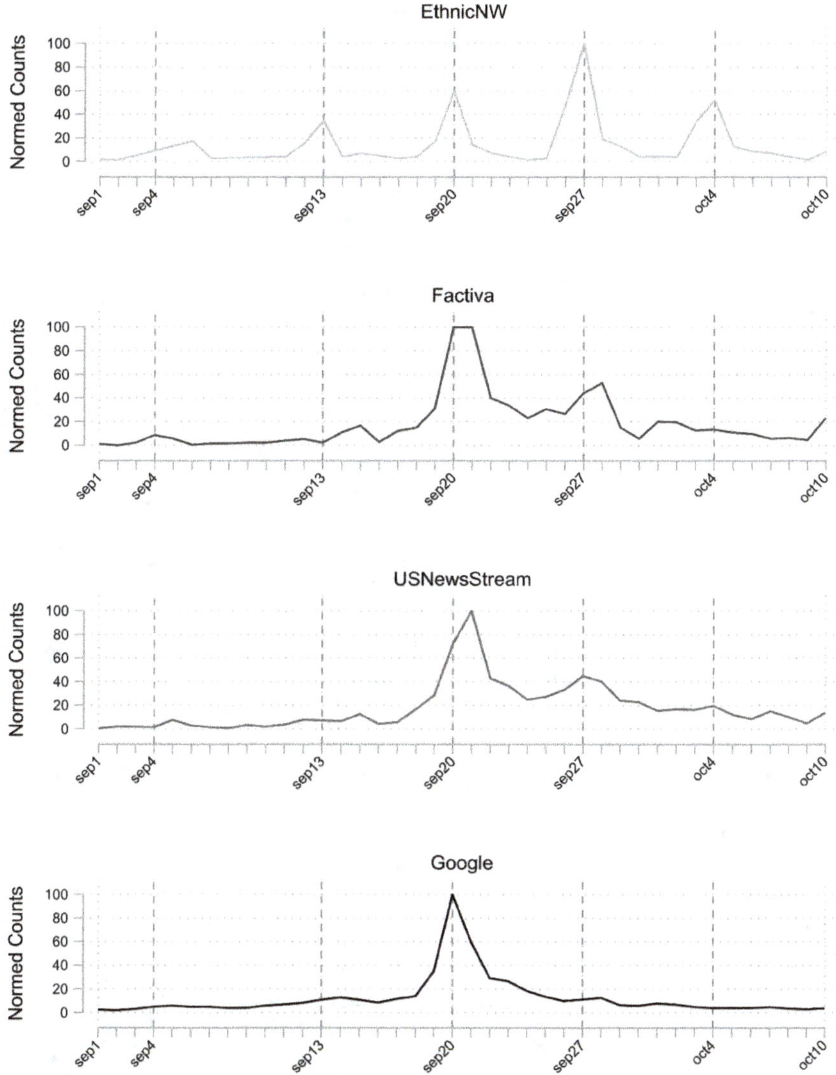

Figure 3 Normed counts of relevant news articles from Ethnic NewsWatch, Factiva, and US NewsStream (top three panels) and of Google searches for Jena (bottom panel) between September 1 and October 10, 2007. Scaled as proportion of maximum within each series, maximum set to 100.

NewsStream was from Louisiana sources. There are a few Black newspaper articles in Ethnic NewsWatch in July and then more attention in August.

Google Trends searches for "Jena" show only small and difficult to measure ripples around a generally low level with a slow rise from mid-June to mid-August. There is a one-day spike in searching for Jena on July 1, the day of the

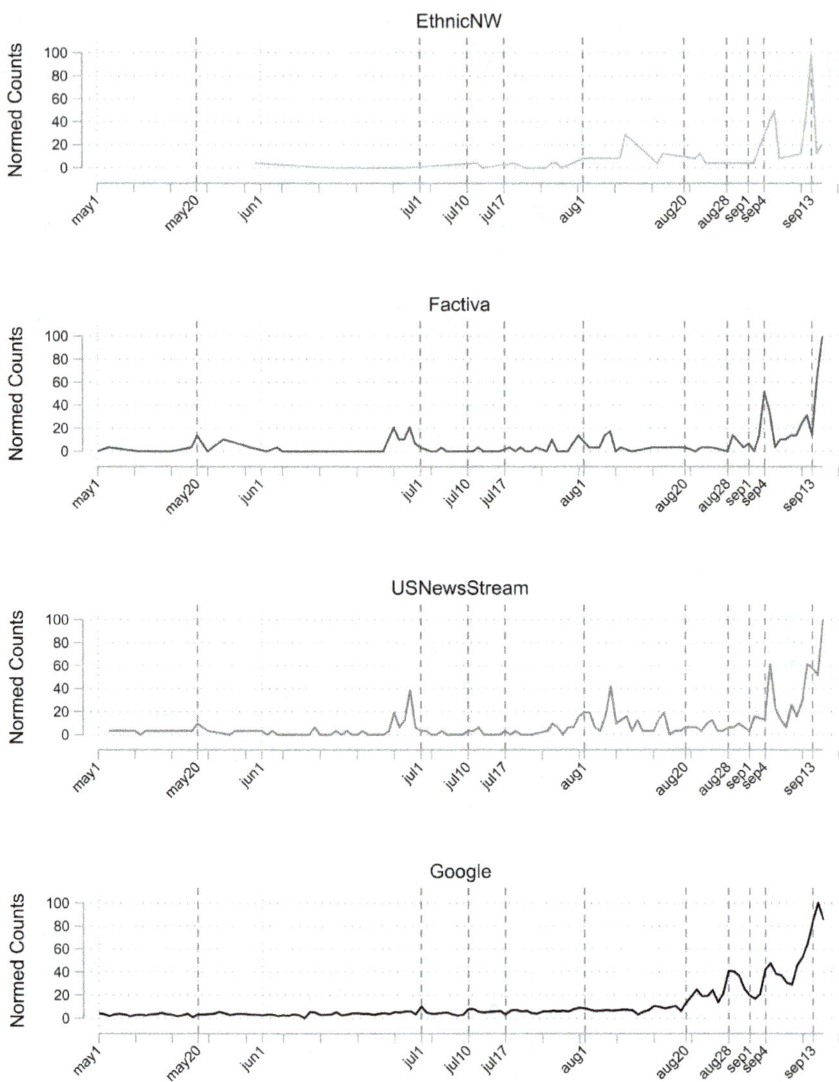

Figure 4 Normed counts of relevant news articles from Ethnic NewsWatch, Factiva, and US NewsStream (top three panels) and of Google searches for Jena (bottom panel) between May 1 and September 15, 2007. Scaled as proportion of maximum within each series, maximum set to 100.

BlackAmericaWeb.com story covering Mychal Bell's trial, a spike for searches for Jena, Jena 6, and Jena Six on July 10, the date of Democracy Now! coverage of the case that featured an interview with Jordan Flaherty and interviews with Jena residents, and possibly a rise for these terms in the two days after July 17 when Color of Change sent its first email about the case. There is a clear rise in

Google Trends for searches for Jena, Jena Six, and Jena 6 that begins on August 20, although this rise is dwarfed by later increases. Two high-circulation weekly magazines published articles about the Jena case on August 20: mainstream *Newsweek* and Black-centric *Jet*. Another rise in Google trends August 28–30 does not seem linked to publications[25] and may be tied to Black radio.

Before mid-August, the Jena case attracted less attention from mainstream and Black media than the Genarlow Wilson case. Although we could find no stories about Jena on the Internet Archive of BlackAmericaWeb.com for the saved dates of July 5, 6, 8, and 11, there are stories about Genarlow Wilson on all those dates, including a report of a protest in Atlanta involving 2000 people. Google Trends comparisons with the keyword Genarlow tell the same story as the media data. Although the search term "Genarlow" has no non-zero baseline, Google Trends reveals a few bursts of attention to Genarlow between January and mid-July that are much larger than the volume of attention given to Jena before September 1. Before late August, Genarlow Wilson was more attention-worthy than the Jena 6.

Bloggers

The AfroSpear[26] was a group of about 100 Black bloggers organized in April 2007 with the intention of contributing to the Black movement by coordinating and amplifying Black news and perspectives among bloggers. In March 2007, Black bloggers had amplified a story by Howard Witt about the case of Shaquanda Cotton, a fourteen-year-old Black girl in Paris, Texas, who was sentenced to up to seven years in juvenile prison for shoving a White school aide. Within four days, Witt's story comparing Cotton's punishment to a White girl who had received probation for arson from the same judge had received 21,000 hits and had been picked up by more than 200 blogs including AfroSpear writers. This contributed to the girl's release by the end of March (Greenlea 2014, 80). Witt's story about her release says "Since the Tribune's first account of Shaquanda Cotton's case, her story has been circulated on more than 400 Internet blogs and featured in newspapers and radio and TV reports across the country. Two protests demanding her release were held in Paris and a third, to be led by Rev. Al Sharpton, was scheduled for Tuesday" (Witt 2007b). This prior experience set up the connection between Witt and the AfroSpear bloggers for the Jena case.

---

[25] The small rise in Factiva counts includes reports that Bell had juvenile convictions, several student newspaper stories, and AP reports that Jena High has banned "Free the Jena 6" T-shirts.

[26] https://afrospear.wordpress.com/.

We spent some time searching for traces of blogs about Jena because of published but unsubstantiated claims that bloggers "were largely responsible for the early reporting on the Jena 6 case" (Payton and Kvasny 2012). The large majority of blogs from that period are not accessible, so our conclusions about the impacts of bloggers cannot be definitive. We could find no evidence of nonlocal blogging about the Jena case before May 20, unless Jordan Flaherty's and Tom Mangold's online articles are counted as blogs. Still-accessible AfroSpear blogs about Jena begin with responses to Witt's May 20 article and quickly reference the Mangold and Flaherty pieces and sometimes the *Town Talk* articles. AfroSpear bloggers continue to write about the case after May 20, but comments on June posts increase markedly in July and August, suggesting rising attention later in the year. Most blog posts cited in other research date from late August or September 2007, not the early organizing period. What we can find is consistent with Greenlea's interviews with AfroSpear bloggers (2014, chapter 2) that they amplified news stories rather than doing original reporting. Some later bloggers did go to Jena and offer original reportage, most notably law professor Bill Quigley's July *Facing South* blog post about Jena.

We compared Google Trends for Shaquanda [Cotton], Genarlow [Wilson], and Jena, Jena Six, and Jena 6. There are bursts of searching for Shaquanda in late March and early April when the case was being discussed by Witt and bloggers. These bursts are much smaller than the Genarlow bursts but much larger than those for Jena Six or Jena 6 through July. The burst of searching for Shaquanda brings it up to the baseline level for searches for Jena. Our analysis of multiple samples from Google Trends can detect no rise in attention to Jena between January and mid-June. There is a slow rise between mid-June and mid-August that might possibly be attributed to bloggers, although news coverage of the trial and growing involvement of national organizations is also happening. The Google Trends rise is punctuated by spikes that seem associated with BlackAmercaWeb and Democracy Now! coverage and the July 31 protest. This modest impact is consistent with AfroSpear bloggers' frustrations (reported by Greenlea) that high-profile White-centric progressive blogs were not sharing their messages.

The Jena campaign was seen at the time as marking the entry of social media into protest campaigns. Alan Bean discussed attention from progressive blogs in his own blogs beginning in May. Abbey Brown discussed bloggers in a June 11 *Town Talk* article, saying that a Google search of "Jena Six" had turned up nearly 1,000 entries without clearly saying that these hits were quoting or requoting the original Flaherty, Mangold, and Witt pieces. Later, Howard Witt and the bloggers themselves expanded the claim and turned bloggers into a causal agent rather than one mechanism for amplifying news media stories.

Phase Three, Late August to September: Call to Protest and the Communication and Mobilization Cascade

The Jena 6 became a huge media cascade centering on the September 20 rally. It appears that it was the call to protest and not the Jena 6 case itself that motivated protesters and drew media and public attention. Most mainstream news coverage was reactive, responding to the protest. Many Black newspapers are published weekly and the peak for Ethnic NewsWatch is September 27, a week after the rally, but Ethnic NewsWatch also shows substantial prospective coverage of the protest the week before the rally, on September 13.

After the July 31 rally, everyone involved expected the next protest date would be Mychal Bell's rescheduled sentencing. *Town Talk* coverage of the July 31 protest quoted Khadijah Rashad from Lafayette's Community Defender television saying, "When there is going to be sentencing again, we need to flood this area with as much people as we possibly can. We want the entire world to know." Al Sharpton said in his early August visit that he would keep coming back until justice is done. An August 15 article by Jordan Flaherty says the families have called for a demonstration on September 20 (Flaherty 2007b). In coverage of Sharpton and King's visit on August 14, Deric Muhammad, a spokesman for the Houston Millions More Movement Ministry of Justice said "The next big event will be on September 20, when Bell is to be sentenced. We are expecting more people than the few hundred who showed up for the first sentencing date of July 31" and that "there is a growing student movement in support of the Jena 6 on college campuses such as LSU, Texas Southern and the University of Michigan" (Shabazz 2007).

It took time for the call to protest in Jena on September 20 to circulate widely into news media. The August 20 *Newsweek* article says, "a host of national figures–from the Rev. Al Sharpton to the Nation of Islam to the American Civil Liberties Union–have descended on the town to inveigh against racial injustice" (Kovach and Campo-Flores 2007). The August 20 *Jet* article discusses Sharpton's visit to Jena and gives even more attention to a Chicago radio show and rally on August 18 featuring Jesse Jackson (Waldron and Chappell 2007). But neither article mentions a September 20 protest. Of the 25 articles archived in Ethnic NewsWatch with August publication dates that mention the Jena case, only one *Amsterdam News* article published on August 16 mentions a September 20 protest. A story in the mainstream Milwaukee *Journal Sentinel* dated September 2 by Black journalist Eugene Kane about the case says, "My e-mail inbox was filled up last week with pleas from activists across the nation to write about the Jena Six," but mentions only the petition campaign and not the call to go to Jena on September 20.

However, communication and organizing were happening. The MMM had gotten people to Jena for July 31 and was organizing in more places through Black college and community groups. Other previously activated groups were also regrouping for a September protest. A blog post by Alan Bean dated August 31 says attendance at a September protest might reach 5000 (FOJ 08–31). Although few sources seem to know about a September 20 protest in August, multiple articles dated September 4 to 6 – mostly in Black newspapers but also in some mainstream outlets – discuss plans for the protest and the involvement of radio hosts.

Although we have no data on the point, most likely messaging through blogs and social media accelerated after the call to protest in mid-August. The fragmentary evidence from the blogs we located shows the greatest activity around publicizing the protest in August and September. Greenlea (2014, 72ff) discusses the content of Black blogging about the case and bloggers' beliefs that they were unusually well poised to coordinate a movement through their decentralized communication structures. Bloggers also communicated via Facebook. Most of the blog content described in academic articles references the protest or events after the protest.

The biggest communication boost probably came via Black radio. Multiple sources say that Michael Baisden was the first radio host to pick up the Jena case and feature it on his show and that the most intense radio coverage of the case was in September. However, we have found no source that says exactly when Michael Baisden first began discussing the case or when radio hosts began publicizing a call to protest on September 20. Google Trends data shows a rise in attention to Jena for August 28 to 30 that is not associated with any published source we have located and may mark the entry of national Black radio to the campaign.

Many at the time credited Black radio hosts and especially Michael Baisden with organizing the rally (Lester and Thomas 2007; Robinson 2007). Michael Baisden said he learned about the Jena case in August about a month after the trial from multiple emails from his listeners (Fears, Thomas-Lester, and Washington Post Staff Writers 2007). He directly encouraged attendance at Jena and claimed credit for tens of thousands of attendees at Jena. Baisden encouraged use of the message board features of his website to create an online ride board, where users could post information about available seats on buses. Baisden collaborated with Al Sharpton, broadcast his show from Jena on September 20, and was the host and main organizer of several events in Alexandria before and after the Jena protests.

The most famous Black radio personality at the time was Tom Joyner, the founder of Reach America, the largest media company covering Black

Americans, which also ran BlackAmericaWeb.com. Joyner had often previously sought to organize support for Black causes. Joyner did not directly seek to mobilize people to attend the Jena protest, but he publicized the case and also decided to broadcast from Jena on the day of the protest. Many of the commentators on Color of Change petitions listed Joyner as a Black leader and said that they heard of the case from him (Greenlea 2014, 137). Baisden, Joyner, and other Black radio hosts allied across network lines to promote the Jena 6 case, mostly in September (Morant 2008, 116–118).

In September the call to protest was circulating through many different Black communication channels: radio, thousands of blogs, Facebook groups with thousands of members, YouTube videos, Black newspapers, and organizational networks including student groups, churches, mosques, and chapters of Black civic and civil rights organizations. These were penetrating social networks and generating feedback as people sought more information. One news article gives an example of the interconnections: "In Memphis, Lashandra Brooks was sitting in the New Direction Christian Church when one of the members stood and talked about Jena. She said there was a YouTube video, and the pastor invited her to show it. 'It got a phenomenal response,' Brooks said. 'People are talking about it in barbershops and hair salons, asking, "Why didn't I know about this earlier?"'" (Fears, Thomas-Lester, and Washington Post Staff Writers 2007). Another example comes from the personal account we received from sociologist Aisha Upton-Azzam, who was a student at the time. She learned about the Jena protest about three weeks in advance from her grandmother, who learned about it on Facebook and paid for Aisha's ticket for the Jena bus from Chicago.

4 Making a Protest and Building a Movement

The media cascade was about the protest, and the evidence is that the desire to be part of a historic event was a major motivation for participants. The call to protest coincides with Al Sharpton bringing other "big name" civil rights leaders to Jena. Black activists with many different ideologies saw this as an opportunity to revive the Black movement. But the big rally was not just a media cascade and communicating about the rally was not enough to make it happen. The event had meaning because people showed up in person to Jena and, to a lesser extent, because they showed up in person to solidarity rallies around the country. Mundane arrangements were crucial, even as they are unlikely to inspire future activists. The Jena rally could happen on short notice because there were standard scripts to follow and organizations on the ground to implement them.

Getting People to Jena

Chartered buses and personal vehicles were the only ways to get to Jena. Chartering buses is a longstanding part of organizing big protests drawing out-of-towners, even those in cities served by trains and planes. Chartered buses are place-based: each makes a round trip from a physical location to the protest and back again. Someone contracts with the bus company, pays a deposit, and either subsidizes the trip or sells tickets for it. Buses were organized by on-the-ground groups or local coalitions of groups. Social media and websites including those organized by James Rucker's ColorOfChange.org and Michael Baisden shared information about available transport organized by on-the-ground groups.

Radio host Michael Baisden claimed to be responsible for most of the crowd, while Greenlea speculates that Rucker and ColorOfChange accounted for most of the attendees. The Millions More Movement, often organizing through Black colleges and often collaborating with local churches, accounted for a large share of the buses coming to Jena. Buses associated with Michael Baisden transported people first to Alexandria and then to Jena. Many other buses bypassed the Alexandria events and traveled directly to Jena, often with passengers eating and sleeping on the buses.

Using news articles from the *Town Talk* and our larger project, we compiled a table of buses to Jena (see Appendix D) that, at 50 a bus, seems to account for about 220 buses or about 11,000 people from 25 cities. Adding one bus from each of another twenty-five cities in accord with MMM's claim of having buses from fifty cities, we get a total minimum of 245 buses and 12,250 people. In its pre-event coverage, the *Los Angeles Sentinel* estimated that there would be a total of 500 to 1,000 buses (and 25,000 to 50,000 people). Given the incompleteness of our tally, it seems plausible that there could have been 500 buses coming to Jena.

Organizations reported to be coordinating buses included Black colleges, the Millions More Movement, the NAACP, NAN, Rainbow/PUSH, Black churches, and many ad hoc local Black coalitions that included Black newspapers, Black radio stations, Black businesses, and Black organizations. Places mentioned in news coverage as sending delegations included New Jersey, New York City, Birmingham, Atlanta, Miami, Charlotte, St. Louis, Philadelphia, Orlando, Houston, Dallas, Southern California, Los Angeles, Detroit, Chicago, Prince George's County Maryland, Washington DC, Durham, Greensboro, Chapel Hill, Columbus (Georgia), Memphis, Columbus (Ohio), Cleveland, Nashville, and the Louisiana cities of Lafayette, Monroe, Baton Rouge, New Orleans, and Shreveport. Black labor unions and the Harlem Revolutionary Club were mentioned as organizing in New York. Local churches in collaboration with other local Black organizations and media outlets were credited with forming the coalitions that organized protesters in Dallas and Nashville (Greenlea 2014, 115–121, 167–172) while Black newspapers and radio stations seemed to be key to the coalition of organizations and volunteers that formed in Los Angeles to fill buses for Jena and provide riders with food. As momentum built, Black people and Black organizations scrambled to get involved. Black newspapers reported the involvement of labor leaders and labor unions and militant Black nationalist or socialist groups that were not mentioned in mainstream sources.

Others came in private transportation. Black motorcycle clubs, whose members were often police or ex-military, came to Jena in groups, especially from nearby cities (Greenlea 2014, 144–156). Many carpooled from around the country, and there was also high attendance via private vehicles from people in the region.

Religious networks provided housing. The *Town Talk* reported that Alexandria churches were hosting two to three thousand people who were coming from churches in thirty-six states. Many other people coming from outside Louisiana slept on their buses. There were also many buses and private vehicles that came into Jena from places within six hours of driving that could treat it as a day trip, including New Orleans, Houston, Dallas, and Memphis as well as the smaller cities in the region.

Solidarity Protests and Movement Building

There were solidarity protests in dozens of cities. Before September 20, at least 2,000 students rallied at Howard University on September 5, about 100 in Chicago on September 5, and an unknown number in San Diego on September 13. Sometime in early September, a group of 40 mayors meeting in Trenton issued a statement about the Jena case. On September 17, a rally of a "large number" of New York City lawmakers and organization leaders was held, and a Chicago minister called for a national day of prayer about the case.

There were gatherings in many cities as the buses left on September 18 and 19, and solidarity gatherings on September 20 for the people staying behind. Our project recorded specific mention of thirty-five events in twenty-two different cities that we estimate involved somewhere between 6500 and 36,000 people[27] plus more vague reports that there were gatherings in many more cities. Many of these events involved Black politicians, Black labor

---

[27] Our event size estimate ranges are broad because most articles did not mention event sizes and we estimate plausible minimum and maximum event sizes from all information in the news stories.

leaders, and Black leaders of local organizations or churches. The Jena mobilization had become a bandwagon that people wanted to be on.

The evidence is that people did the work to get people to Jena and to solidarity rallies because they saw the potential for movement building. Prominent New York Black radio host Bob Law argued that local Black leaders around the country were important for mobilizing people: "You can't say enough about the job Michael Baisden did. He heightened the awareness of Black people who don't normally participate in these types of demonstrations ... There was Kwame Kenyatta in Detroit, Chokwe Lumumba in Mississippi with the Katrina Tribunal, Zaki Baruti in St. Louis, Cynthia McKinney in Atlanta and the Malcolm X Grassroots Movement through their chapters across the country ... There has been a new leadership created as a result of the Jena 6 mobilization."

Planning and Confusion

Local news reports said authorities were not sure what the protesters' plans were and that those granted permits to protest in Jena on Thursday were: National Association for the Advancement of Colored People, Louisiana Legislative Black Caucus, National Black Caucus, National Bar Association, Michael Baisden Show, Rainbow/PUSH, and the National Action Network. However, the two main groups organizing events were the Louisiana NAACP in collaboration with other groups and leaders (and including Al Sharpton) and Michael Baisden in collaboration with Al Sharpton.

Representatives of major civil rights organizations and radio host Michael Baisden cobbled together some advance planning for the rally. The established civil rights organizations attempted to coordinate efforts even though there was tension between groups operating in Jena. One faction included the regional groups that had been active since the previous spring, including Alan Bean, the ACLU, and the NAACP, who worked most closely with Caseptla Bailey and were tied to other activists with regional ties including James Rucker. The other faction was centered on Al Sharpton, who had been contacted by Mychal Bell's family via the prior involvement of Raymond Brown from New Orleans NAN. Sharpton was tied to radio hosts Tom Joyner and Michael Baisden as well as other national-level activists with no local connections including Martin Luther King III and Jesse Jackson.

Staging for the protest was in Alexandria, 40 miles away, where the city officially welcomed the protesters. Months before, the state convention of the Louisiana NAACP had been scheduled for Alexandria; going to the protest was added to the convention agenda. Al Sharpton and others announced that they did not want to spend money in Jena and Jena merchants were fearful of the crowds and generally closed their businesses, but it is inconceivable that so many people could have been housed and fed in Jena anyway. Hotels were full throughout the region. Many protesters ate and slept in their buses. Others came in RV's or camped out.

Michael Baisden hosted a rally in Alexandria on September 19 at the Levee Park Amphitheatre from 11:00 am to 6:00 pm and then broadcast his radio show live from an event at the Riverfront Center in the evening with $10 ticket sales going to support the Jena Six defense and Al Sharpton speaking. About 1500 people attended that event. Tickets for the bus ride to Jena were also on sale. On September 20, Baisden's plan was that his buses would leave Alexandria at 5:30 am. In fact, they did not leave until after 7:00 am and many had not reached Jena by 9:00, when the courthouse rally started. After the Jena events, Baisden hosted another rally back in Alexandria that began at noon with hundreds attending and crowds growing during the day as people returned from Jena.

The *Jena Times* and the Alexandria *Town Talk* published multiple articles about the advance arrangements and logistics on the day of the protest. Local governments declared an emergency in hopes of obtaining state and federal funding for arrangements. Hundreds of law enforcement officers came from agencies around Louisiana to help manage the event. Local governments provided portable toilets. The Red Cross provided first aid stations, water, and snacks.

The original plan by civil rights groups including NAACP, Rainbow/PUSH, the SCLC, and NAN was to assemble in Jena beginning at 6:00 am at the Ward 10 Recreation Center about two miles south of the courthouse, a largely wooded area in the unincorporated part of town where most of the Black residents lived. (See Jena map in Figure 1.) The plan was to march to the courthouse, rally, and march back. This would feed into a planned hip-hop concert at the Recreation Center in the afternoon and evening. Concert organizer Catrina Wallace, Robert Bailey's sister, said the concert would benefit the legal expenses of the Jena 6 and "bring together the young people of Jena and surrounding communities with local artists and performers from around the country," and share a vision for young people, families, and communities achieving justice and equity. Alan Bean claimed that the NAACP did not publicize and tried to block the concert due to offensive language in hip hop music (FOJ 09–23).

Baisden and Sharpton pulled out of the original plan after Michael Baisen's aide visited the site on September 17 and reported that the park was too small and isolated for the expected crowds and the planned march too long. Baisden said later that the march between the park and courthouse was canceled in a conference call that evening. The civil rights coalition wanted to continue to rally at the Recreation Center, but Baisden said later he refused to endorse that plan because the crowds would not fit there and he thought a march past Jena High was important. The main rally remained scheduled for 9:00 am at the courthouse, but other plans for assembly and marching were not coordinated. Some protesters associated with the NAACP assembled at the Recreation Center, held a rally, and marched to the courthouse from there, while the Baisden buses went directly to the courthouse.

Disorganization, Standard Templates, and Meaning

On the day of the rally, there were too many people trying to fit into in a small space. The mass media were there in force, with television crews from the major networks and reporters from a wide variety of mainstream, progressive, and Black-centric organizations. Many Black radio hosts were there. The small group of activists who had been working in Jena for months were sidelined, while the media focused on the Jena 6 families and the celebrities.

By 5:00 am the roads were already crowded and the lawn by the courthouse was already filling up. There were Muslim and Christian prayers at sunrise. Some people gathered at the Ward 10 Recreation Center according to the original plan and rallied there. The rally at the courthouse began on time at 9:00 am even though many of the buses from Alexandria had still not arrived. Traffic was backed up for miles. After the rally, a faction led by Al Sharpton and Mychal Bell's mother Melissa Bell marched from the courthouse to the high school, then to the junior high, and then to the town park. Many protesters were met by buses at the park, while others marched back to the courthouse and met buses there. Many marched or wandered around the town in their own groups, holding smaller spontaneous rallies at various locations. Although there had been an agreement between protest organizations and the authorities that no one would go on the Jena High School grounds, there was no way to enforce this agreement and many people entered the school grounds and conducted their own rallies there. Chokwe Lumumba, one of the founders of Malcolm X Grassroots Movement who later was elected mayor of Jackson, Mississippi, spoke at one of the impromptu rallies at the school.

Only a few thousand people could fit in the courthouse area and most people marched or milled around in other parts of Jena. There were many speakers at the 9:00 am rally but no news article mentioned more than a few. Besides Al Sharpton, Michael Baisden and Tom Joyner (who were broadcasting from the rally), those mentioned as speaking in the articles we read included Robert Muhammad (Southwest Regional Minister of the Nation of Islam), Mychal Bell's grandmother Rosey Simmons and cousin Tiffany, rappers Mos Def and

Ice Cube, New Orleans Mayor Ray Nagin, Alabama State Senator Bobby Singleton, comedians George Wilborn and Ricky Smiley, an African drummer, someone reading from the Rev. Dr. Martin Luther King Jr.'s "I have a dream" speech, and someone from the New Black Panther Party ending the rally with a chant: "We're nonviolent when people are nonviolent with us, We're not nonviolent with people that are violent with us." What was newsworthy was that there was a protest, not what the speakers said. News articles focused on interviews with protesters and their motivations for coming and described most protesters as checking their phones, taking selfies, and talking to other protesters, not focusing on the speeches. The mood of the crowd was described as both festive and solemn.

Nearly all protesters had left Jena by noon. Only a few hundred remained in the courthouse area through the afternoon and a few hundred were gathered at the Ward 10 Recreation Center into the evening. It seems unlikely that the out-of-town protesters even knew about the planned concert at the Recreation Center.

Two things stand out. One, despite all the disorganization, the gathering in Jena was entirely peaceful. The hundreds of law enforcement officers from around the state who had been deployed to the event handled traffic and chatted amiably with protesters. Both protesters and law enforcement were following a template for a peaceful gathering. The only problems were heat-related illnesses in a few hundred marchers. Most Jena residents either left town or stayed indoors. The few who came out to interact with the protesters either agreed with them or conducted civil conversations about their disagreements. A couple of Jena residents who insulted the protesters were shushed by their neighbors.

Second, despite both the standard template and the disorganization, the event was meaningful as a protest. It demonstrated Black solidarity and support for the Jena 6 just by happening. It did not really matter what people did in Jena; the simple fact that they had gotten themselves to Jena made a statement. It was understood as a historic event by both the participants and the media. It was being there that mattered. News coverage compared it to the marches of the Civil Rights era and discussed whether this represented the revival of the Civil Rights Movement. The number of attendees was substantially smaller than the several hundred thousand who had attended the October 2005 Millions More Movement rally in Washington DC, but there was much more news coverage of the Jena rally, and it was treated in both mainstream and Black news sources as much more significant. Its power as a movement story came from its relative spontaneity compared to big rallies planned months in advance and the perception that it was a movement from below of ordinary people, not an orchestrated event from an established organization.

Narratives of Movement Building

With the advantage of hindsight, the Jena 6 protest looks like a turning point and bridge between a movement organized in the wake of the Civil Rights Movement and what became the Black Lives Movement of the 2010s. It is the last big Black movement event following the solidaristic model built around the 1995 Million Man March. It was seen at the time as a potential opening to a new wave of Black activism, as welcoming a new generation into the ongoing Black movement. Both mainstream and Black news sources[28] drew comparisons between the Jena protest and Civil Rights protests of the 1960s. Both mainstream and Black news sources quoted Al Sharpton saying that this could be the beginning of the 21st Century civil rights movement that would challenge racial disparities in the justice system. Although both source types discussed the idea that the new movement would focus on the criminal justice system, this emphasis was more common in Black newspapers.

While no newswire articles mentioned any precedents from after 1965, a few Black newspaper articles said it was the most important Black event since the historic 1995 Million Man March. The only mention we saw of the 2005 Millions More Movement rally was one activist who was quoted as drawing a comparison between the two events, saying, "There were more young people, lots of college students and even younger. The response to the incident to me represents and signals the changing of the guard." This theme of the awakening of a new generation was echoed in many Black newspaper articles.

The Jena rally inspired mass participation because it was seen as a historic event that would demonstrate Black solidarity and inspire a new movement generation. Both mainstream newswires and Black newspapers gave many examples of people bringing their children and grandchildren to the rally and quoted young people as wanting to be part of history: "This is the first time something like this has happened for our generation. . . . You always heard about it from history books and relatives. This is a chance to experience it for ourselves" (*New York Times*) and "It was a good chance to be part of something historic since I wasn't around for the civil rights movement. This is kind of the 21st century version of it" (*Sacramento Observer*). The emphasis on general awareness of discrimination, importance of collective action, concern with justice, and learning form history – not just the specific case of the Jena 6 – was also evident in the essays written by students of an HBCU as a requirement for their bus ride to Jena (C. Gibson and Williams 2020).

As political scientist and founder of Black Youth Project Cathy Cohen wrote in 2010: "For many in black communities, mobilization around the Jena 6

---

[28] See Appendix C.

reignited the hope that black politics – as it is often imagined and conceptualized: that is, extrasystemic, collective, movement politics – is still alive among the younger generation of black Americans" (Cohen 2010, 151). The Jena mobilization was seen at the time as potentially opening a new wave of Black activism. Although both mainstream newswires and Black newspapers highlighted young people seeing this as the movement of their generation, Black newspapers were more likely than mainstream newswires to use the words "young," "youth," and "generation" and much more often emphasized the idea that the older generation wanted the younger generation to become involved. A high school senior was quoted saying: "The adult community always tells us that maybe we should as students get out there and do something positive. By this being our own initiative, we're actually proving that we do care about our community, nation, our rights and protecting them the best way we can." Black newspapers often quoted older adult activists stressing the importance of the younger generation waking up and getting involved. Here are several examples:

- Jeri Wright, president of the Chicago chapter of the National Action Network: "The next generation has come face-to-face with racism. . . Now they are part of the movement in their day and age speaking out against a grave injustice."
- Adult supporter Tonette Moore: "We also need to get our young people involved and pass on social awareness to them."
- Carol Hall, 63, a retired government worker: "Until now, the majority of young Black people felt they were so advanced with their i-Pods, cell phones, computers and other electronic media [they believed] that racial problems did not exist anymore. When they removed those iPod ear buds from their ears, they began to hear the cry of their ancestors, the Scottsboro Boys, the Little Rock 9 and on up to the modern day Don Imus calling their Black sisters bitches and hos."
- Nigel Parkinson, a business man: "Black people can never get complacent and say it's not in our neighborhood. Some young people may feel that Martin Luther King, Jr. did it all. But young people are waking up now."
- Rev. Joseph Lowery, a cofounder of the SCLC: ". . . there's a real awakening, a long prayed for awakening among our youth. No matter how much adults try to take credit for organizing and doing this, this came up out of the bosom and the belly of our youth. And I say thank God."
- Myrlie Evers-Williams: "I have emphasized the need for communication between the two generations, that those of us who are experienced in the struggle for freedom need to reach out more than what we do to embrace the new leadership that's coming along. We've got to come together to use the

wisdom of the past and the enthusiasm of today to still address these ills that face our society."

Dorothy Height of the National Council of Negro Women, Mark Potok of The Intelligence Project, NAACP Chairman Julian Bond, and Willie Barrow of Rainbow/PUSH were also quoted as stressing the need for a new movement. A report on a panel discussion in Philadelphia after the rally stressed the importance of helping youth connect present events with history and understand the need to become more involved. There were also multiple reports of teachers taking their students to local solidarity rallies.

Mainstream newswires were largely done with covering the campaign within a week, except for covering the later rallies. By contrast, Black newspapers published many post-rally articles around the theme of "What do we do next?" and "Now what?" These articles either reflected on the prospects for a resurgence of the movement or provided information on what people were doing to build a new movement and inviting them to participate. For example, the *Amsterdam News* quoted Bob Law, activist, radio talk show host, and the New York chair of the Millions More Movement as saying that some were surprised at the expression of unity in the Jena protest, stressing the creation of new leadership from the movement, and inviting people to a meeting for organizing.

Follow-Up, Dispersal, and Reverberations

Black activists sought to keep the momentum going after the big rally. On September 25, Mychal Bell's parents and Al Sharpton met with Congressional Black Caucus leaders asking them to hold hearings about the case. The Congressional Black Caucus urged outgoing Louisiana governor Kathleen Blanco to pardon the Jena 6, but she did not. Solidarity protests for the Jena 6 continued for a few weeks after September 20. There was a call for a national student walkout on October 1 that was supported by rapper Mos Def (Cole 2008); our data include reports of three small protests (involving dozens or hundreds of participants) in Pittsburgh, New York, and DC on October 1 and 2 and a few forums discussing the issues raised by the case.

There was an unusually high number of reports about noose hangings and other symbolic hate crimes in the fall of 2007 (Oliver et al. 2022) as well as extensive reportage about an FBI report released in the fall of 2007 about rising hate crimes in 2006. On October 16, the House Judiciary Committee held a hearing about the Jena 6 case and related issues, with most of the discussion focusing on how the nooses should have been handled and some discussion of issues of unfair prosecution ("Jena Six Case | C-SPAN.org" 2007). For over a decade, October 22 had been a national day of Black rallies against police violence; the Jena case was folded into the rallies held in several cities on that day, including one in New York.

Al Sharpton and other Civil Rights leaders organized a protest in Washington on November 16 that linked the Jena 6 case to broader issues of criminal injustice and called for stronger penalties for hate crimes, especially noose hangings. About 50,000 people attended the rally – probably more than had gone to Jena – and thousands attended a linked free concert the next day. This rally received much less news coverage than the Jena rally. President Bush was pressured to say that he thought noose hanging should be a crime.

And then the protest episode was largely over. Despite all the grassroots energy, and the flurry of follow-up rallies around the country, the mobilization around the Jena 6 dissipated almost as quickly as it had built.

What happened next was the 2008 presidential campaign of Barack Obama and the election of the first Black president. Although there are no studies that examine the question directly, there are scholarly speculations that the youthful energy around the Jena 6 mobilization found its next expression in the Obama campaign. In reflecting on the Jena 6 campaign and continuing the quotation from above, Cathy Cohen said that instead of a traditional protest movement, the participation of the new generation could be seen in voter engagement and other forms of action and organizing, including online organizing: "Ironically, despite data indicating that young black Americans spurred an increase in youth voting in the 2004 presidential elections and in 2008 had the highest turnout of young people among any ethnic or racial group since 1972, when talking about politics, it is the spectacle of mass mobilization that seems to hold the imagination of both young and old in black communities" (Cohen 2010, 151).

The path from 2008 to the explosion of BLM protests beginning in 2014 goes through the Obama campaign, Michelle Alexander's 2010 book *The New Jim Crow*,[29] disillusionment with the Obama presidency and his failure to intervene in the 2011 execution of Troy Davis (Taylor 2016), the Occupy movement of 2011 (Taylor 2016; Weddington 2022, 2024) and the publicity and protests around the Trayvon Martin killing in 2012 and the not guilty verdict of George Zimmerman in 2013, which led not only to the often-cited creation of the #BlackLivesMatter hashtag (and later organization of the same name) but also the formation of another important organization, BYP100 (BYP100 2018; Simpson, Walter, and Ebert 2021), at a meeting of Cohen's Black Youth Project. Although nobody called the new wave of Black protests a "civil rights movement," Al Sharpton did get it right in 2007 when he said that the next round of the Black movement was

---

[29] Alan Bean used the phrase "new Jim Crow" often in his 2007 blogs. Alexander discusses the Jena Six protest and its "old" Jim Crow framing in her book but makes no mention of Alan Bean or his use of "new Jim Crow" to describe modern injustices in the criminal legal system.

going to be focused on the criminal justice system. The people who were aged eighteen in 2007 were twenty-five in 2014, when the BLM protests erupted. The new generation was taking over the movement. How that happened must be the subject of a different research project, but the Jena protest marks the end of one era and the beginning of the next.

5 Aftermath

Attention to the Jena case provoked racist backlash. There was a great deal of news coverage of the arrest in Alexandria of two young men for displaying a noose on their pickup truck and taunting people returning from the Alexandria rallies, generally the only mention of Alexandria in non-local coverage of the Jena rallies. The day after the rally, the FBI announced that a neo-Nazi in Virginia had posted the names and addresses of the Jena 6 on his web site with the headline "Lynch the Jena 6." The families received hundreds of threatening calls. Justin Barker gave an interview to a White supremacist group, but later said he'd been duped by them and did not know who they were. The *Town Talk* online forum – at that time unmoderated –included many hate-filled comments and the newspaper received daily hostile and threatening phone calls, including death threats to reporter Abbey Brown. Members of the New Black Panther Party announced they would provide security for the families and other Black residents of Jena in collaboration with other groups, including the Millions More Movement and the Black Muslims.

On January 21, 2008 – MLK Day – about fifty White supremacists from the Mississippi-based Nationalist Movement held a rally at the LaSalle County courthouse in Jena and were met by about 100 counterdemonstrators. Al Sharpton preached at a church in Jena on the Sunday before but was not at the counterdemonstration on Monday.

As outside attention grew in 2007, the biracial ministerial alliance in Jena had collapsed. In February 2008, Jena Baptist churches began what was initially planned as a one-week revival that lasted eight weeks and, in the last two weeks, moved into spaces in the Black part of town and included themes of racial reconciliation. One of the key participants was Rev. Jimmy Young, pastor of L&A Missionary Baptist Church, where the first protest about the nooses had been held. On the first anniversary of the big protest, Rev. Young and other ministers were quoted as saying they thought the events had improved racial issues by forcing them to pay attention to community needs.

Robert Bailey's mother Caseptla Bailey and his sister Catrina Wallace, who had organized local protests in Jena in the first half of 2007, stayed in Jena after the big rally and founded Organizing in the Trenches, a community organization focused on empowering youth, but they struggled to obtain funding after national attention turned away. In July 2009, Catrina Wallace was one of a dozen people arrested in a big "drug bust" in Jena that was highlighted in a press conference held by the sheriff. No drugs were found in her home, or the homes of other arrestees, but she was held on a $150,000 cash-only bond and her car was impounded. The case was viewed by many as retaliation for the 2007 protests. Wallace was sentenced to prison in 2011; her sentences were vacated on appeal in 2014 on the grounds of judicial excess in sentencing. In 2015, she was found murdered alongside her employer in a Monroe bail bond firm.

Consequences for the Jena 6

Attention to the six Jena youths themselves largely died down within a month, except for controversies about whether they had misspent the money raised on their behalf. Mychal Bell's conviction in adult court for felonious assault had been overturned by appeals court the week before the big rally, although he was still in jail. Bell was released from jail on September 28 after a donor put up $5400 to cover the bond and was met by Al Sharpton and Martin Luther King III along with media and friends and family. He was then reincarcerated for being in violation of his probation from juvenile convictions. The other five were all out on bail. The legal goal had been met: all the youths now had competent legal counsel.

Mychal Bell pled guilty to a charge of misdemeanor battery in December 2007 as a juvenile and was sentenced to eighteen months of incarceration and given credit for the year he had already spent incarcerated. Reports said that his attorneys were divided about whether Bell should plead guilty or continue to delay the case and risk a harsher sentence, and that there was a desire to get it over with and allow Bell to have a definite release date. In January of 2008, Bell was moved to a foster home for the remainder of his sentence, which was scheduled to end in July, although the Jena judge kept trying to extend his period of supervision. He was allowed to attend school and was reported to be doing well and graduated from high school but was denied permission to play football while there. In December 2008, he was arrested for shoplifting and attempted suicide after the arrest. In August 2011 he was on the Southern University (Baton Rouge) football team (Foster 2011) and graduated from college in 2014.

The attorneys for the other five continued to delay the case with motions and won the removal of the original judge from the case in 2008. These cases were finally resolved in 2009 by plea bargains in which they pled "no contest" to misdemeanors punished by probation and restitution for Barker's medical expenses. They also signed a statement that they had not heard Justin Barker using racial slurs before Mychal Bell hit him. Although news accounts emphasized the lack of incarceration time, it should be remembered that Theo Shaw had been held in adult jail for eight months, and Robert Bailey for five months.

Theo Shaw finished his high school course work at a school outside of Jena and was awarded a Jena High School diploma. He maintained that he was not involved in the fight and with legal help was able to get his record expunged. He graduated from the University of Louisiana Monroe in 2012, interned with the Southern Poverty Law Center in 2014, and attended law school at the University of Washington, where he gave the commencement address in 2018. He clerked for Justice Johnson of the Supreme Court of Louisiana and passed the bar in 2019. He is now a public defender in the District of Columbia.

After his release on bail, Robert Bailey moved to Georgia to live with his father and stepmother to attend high school. He was permitted to play football there and made the honor roll. His supporters emphasized the value of getting him out of the hostile environment of Jena. He graduated from Grambling State University, where he was a member of the ROTC. He joined the army in 2014. In 2017 it was reported that he had earned a masters in sports management and was working as a football coach at the University of Arkansas Pine Bluff.

Bryant Purvis was bailed out quickly and moved to Texas, where he lived with an uncle and went to school. He was arrested in Texas in 2008 for assault. He attended Grambling State University where he played basketball. In 2015 he was living in Dallas and had written a book and was speaking about his experiences; a 2017 report described a book talk at a Louisiana library and his goal of developing a business. He continued to maintain he had not been involved in the fight.

Jesse Beard was arrested again in 2007 for simple battery and assault. To give him a chance for a fresh start, with the cooperation of his mother, one of the Southern Poverty Law Center lawyers became his guardian and Beard moved to the northeast to attend boarding school. He later attended Hofstra University.

Carwin Jones had completed his high school requirements before the fight and was awarded a diploma from Jena High in 2007 and moved out of Jena. He was arrested again in 2008 for misdemeanor simple battery. He declined to speak to reporters for follow-up interviews.

Justin Barker, the victim in the fight, continued to live in Jena. In 2011, he was working on an oil rig (Foster 2011).

6 Conclusions: Narratives and Movement Building

Many actors claimed or were given credit for the Jena campaign including Alan Bean, Michael Baisden, Black radio hosts generally, Al Sharpton, the NAACP, Jordan Flaherty, James Rucker and ColorOfChange.org, bloggers (named and unnamed), and social media. Others who played important roles were less often credited, including the Juvenile Justice Project, Tory Pegram and King Downing of the ACLU, the Nation of Islam and the Millions More Movement, Black colleges and college students, Black churches, and journalists Howard Witt, Tom Mangold, Abbey Brown, and Mary Foster. We showed that all these mattered as they interacted with and reinforced each other.

We showed how the campaign unfolded in three phases. First, regional activists were recruited and organized locally and launched a media campaign that succeeded in getting people active and gaining attention but failed to prevent the unjust conviction of Mychal Bell. Second, after the conviction, the campaign nationalized and brought in more outside support. This phase largely succeeded in its stated objective: the Jena 6 had competent legal counsel by the end of July. However, the processes that would lead to the third phase were in motion. The noose-fight narrative was striking a resonant chord. Mychal Bell had been convicted and his parents reached out to Al Sharpton, who came to town in August. A protest had been called for September. National-level Black activists recognized that the case provided a possibility for movement-building. The third phase was the communications-participation cascade which centered as much or more on the historic opportunity to revive the Black movement as on the specifics of the Jena case.

Our argument is that what activists can control are the kind of ordinary activities we see in phases one and two of the Jena campaign. These efforts happen on a field where there are not only opponents but also other clusters of allied activists promoting other cases. Individual cases of injustice to some extent compete for attention in the national field. Success is not assured and a scale shift to a communication and participation cascade is extremely unlikely. In our account, as valiant as they were and as successful as they were in achieving outside support in phase two, the efforts of Alan Bean, Jordan Flaherty, Howard Witt, the NAACP, and even ColorOfChange.org and Al Sharpton were not sufficient to ensure the phase three cascade.

Polletta and others emphasize the importance of simple open-ended narratives that invite participation for movement building. Academics also prefer simple theoretical narratives built around one main theoretical idea. The narrative we have constructed is more like a convoluted novel about ordinary life with subplots and a surprise twist. The existing activist networks provide the backbone of the story. Jena residents knew about the NAACP and NAN. The Juvenile Justice Network brought in Alan Bean. Local organizing pulled in the ACLU. There were ties among progressive activists and journalists who had been impacted and displaced by hurricane Katrina. James Rucker of ColorOfChange.org (who had Louisiana ties) was drawn in through existing activist and journalist network contacts. The media campaign ran alongside and interacted with the activist connections. Although the initial news stories were recruited, journalists Jordan Flaherty, Howard Witt, and Abbey Brown stuck with the story and their reports (along with those of AP's Mary Foster) about the unfairness of Mychal Bell's trial were important for the transition to a national campaign. Al Sharpton later showed up when asked, as he had for many other local campaigns.

Some of the connections were serendipitous. A Democracy Now broadcast that featured Jordan Flaherty led a member of the Nation of Islam to contact Jesse Muhammad and thereby draw in the NOI and the grassroots infrastructure of the Millions More Movement. Others came in from outside the core networks. Al Sharpton might have responded to appeals from Mychal Bell's family without mediation, but Raymond Brown from New Orleans NAN had shown up in Jena multiple times and was credited with bringing Sharpton into the campaign. Al Sharpton, in turn, brought in civil rights leaders with no local connections and attracted more national-level news coverage. The involvement of Sharpton and other national-level leaders probably influenced Tom Joyner and Michael Baisden's decisions to get involved.

There is agreement that the noose-fight narrative was a powerful part of the Jena campaign, especially as it tied the symbol of the violence of Jim Crow White supremacy with the violence of the "new Jim Crow" of the criminal legal system. We looked more closely at the circulating narrative for what it said about movement-building. Our analysis of the way the noose-fight narrative was shaped in news accounts shows that it not only included the nooses as a symbol of the historic violence of White supremacy, but it erased documented adult collective actions and replaced them with embellished accounts of student protests and even portrayed the fights as individualized acts of resistance to White supremacy. This embellished narrative could be understood as a call to action for the younger generation.

Many of the movement-building narratives that circulated similarly falsely claimed that traditional adult activist organizations and mainstream media had ignored the issue. These narratives erased the media campaign and other mundane networking actions that built the Jena campaign in phases one and two. Claims that bloggers built the movement seem to have been promoted primarily by journalists whose articles had been amplified by bloggers. Claims that Michael Baisden and other radio hosts built the movement erase the grassroots organizing work of the Millions More Movement and the organizational infrastructures of traditional civil rights groups and local Black institutions. The academic focus on the power of the noose-fight narrative for inspiring the mobilization also emphasizes individuals' spontaneous responses and erases the work that went into constructing and deploying that narrative and organizing around it.

As powerful as narratives of spontaneity may be for motivating participation, theorizing and activist practice are better built on more accurate narratives. Accurate narratives show the interplay of mundane actions and unexpected outcomes. Collective action does not magically happen. Someone organizes it. Skills and routines matter. This does not make organizing mechanical or predictable. Movement activists operate in inherently uncertain and complex environments. They cannot achieve their objectives solely by their own efforts: they need to persuade others to join their actions. They are simultaneously coordinating with others and competing with them for attention and support. They have opponents who are trying to block or counter their efforts. Their outcomes are often affected by external circumstances beyond their control. There is no recipe that will assure success. Big successes often arise unexpectedly from people doing their ordinary work of trying to deal with cases of injustice and build movement capacity. These principles can be seen operating in all three phases of the Jena 6 campaign.

What about the transition from phase two to three, from ordinary organization to the scale shift and media cascade? We think the tipping point occurred when national activists saw the potential for movement building. Most of the Black activists involved in seeking support for the Jena 6 were also interested in building movement capacity. The NAACP wanted a local chapter formed. The NAACP, the bloggers, ColorOfChange.org, the Millions More Movement, and Al Sharpton all were trying in their own ways to build more lasting and general structures to support Black collective action and influence.

Al Sharpton's visit to Jena in the first week of August at the request of Mychal Bell's parents is the bridge between routine organizing and the cascade. Sharpton often responded to requests to show up and help draw outside media attention to local Black protests about cases of injustice. As much as there are complaints about "celebrity activism," the truth is that the celebrities do help attract mainstream news attention to an issue. A visit from Al Sharpton or Jesse Jackson generally attracted news coverage but did not generally set off a media cascade, and it did not do so in this case. Our data show a small burst of media attention to the Sharpton visit that then dies down, while there is no detectable response in Google Trends.

The shift happens as the plans for a September 20 protest are announced. Sharpton returned to Jena on August 14 bringing Martin Luther King III with him and reported that Jesse Jackson would also be coming later. Other sources announce a September protest at about the same time. The tipping point in

Google Trends seems to be August 20, when two large circulation national magazines – one mainstream, one Black – covered the story with reports emphasizing the involvement of Sharpton and Jackson. The next burst is August 28–30, which could be when Michael Baisden first got involved. By the first week in September, the big news story is the upcoming protest.

Actions oriented toward generalizing the campaign into movement building had been underway since July and took off as the Jena 6 narrative merged with a call for a national protest. The nooses as a symbol of Jim Crow racist violence came also to signify the movement against Jim Crow and to be linked with a new movement against the modern traumas of mass incarceration and legal injustice. The Jena 6 case came to epitomize the modern struggle with its links to the historic struggles.

Black activists and organizations joined the bandwagon about this case rather than all the other cases of criminal injustice because they saw this as an opportunity for movement revival. Younger people saw it as a generational moment and wanted to be there to be part of it. Older people wanted the younger people to become excited and involved. The moment was happening in cyberspace, but it was also happening in in-person student groups and churches and unions and clubs. Once the message was spreading, it was spreading through multiple channels: radio, social media, Black newspapers. It was spreading through in-person presentations and conversations in churches and fraternal and social organizations. It was these on-the-ground place-based organizations that had the capacity to get people to Jena.

It is important to notice the implications of how the communication and protest cascade happened. First, it involved radio, a popular Black-centric communication medium that focused on Black interests and was centralized so that one message could be sent to millions of people at once. Second, Black people were not just an audience but already had extensive in-person and social media networks so that the message could spread through multiple channels and became endemic. There was already a social and organizational infrastructure in Black communities that could support action. Black movement organizations with genuine social, political, and ideological differences already had established routines of collaborating in Black solidarity events. Third, grassroots organizing preceded the communication cascade, especially MMM outreach to college groups. Fourth, there was little innovation. It was a feat to get people to a remote rural town, but it used existing technologies of chartering buses and forming carpools. Organizations followed well-understood scripts for planning rallies. There was also little ideological innovation. The message drew on prior understandings.

It is wrong to read backward from a case that became a media cascade to argue that it should have been a media cascade earlier. In linking the case to historic oppression and violence, the noose-fight narrative was more powerful than most narratives about overcharging, but it did not set off the cascade. In fact, it got less attention than another overcharging story for most of the summer of 2007. The story that attracted Black enthusiasm and ultimately attracted mainstream media was that thousands of Black people were organizing around going to Jena. That story did not exist until September.

The Jena 6 narrative itself did not attract participation. Intentional actors saw the narrative as an opportunity for movement building. The journalists and bloggers who covered the case in the early months were simultaneously invested in building their reputations and influence and in promoting a story that others were not telling, with the AfroSpear bloggers and progressive activist writers like Jordan Flaherty also intending to promote movement-building. James Rucker of ColorOfChange.org was looking for an issue that would demonstrate the power of his approach. Al Sharpton was trying to build his own influence even as he also sought to bring attention to cases of injustice. Michael Baisden, Tom Joyner, and other radio hosts were seeking to build their audiences while also seeking to advance the broader Black movement.

The timing also seems significant. There had been a resurgence of Black collective grievance in the mishandling of hurricane Katrina and extensive discussions of trying to build or rebuild a Black movement in 2005. Many Black people commented on the 2006 immigration rallies and asked whether Black people were going to get reorganized. There was a widespread desire to find a cause to rally around. In 2007 Barack Obama was already often in the news as a frontrunner in the presidential race as potentially the first Black president.

After the big rally, Black activist organizers tried to build on the enthusiasm generated by the Jena campaign to keep the momentum and rebuild a movement. That it did not happen does not mean they were not trying to make it happen. Mos Def and other Hip Hop artists called for school walkouts and protest rallies. Besides Congressional hearings, Al Sharpton organized a large protest in DC that centered hate crimes and nooses. The Millions More Movement had the explicit agenda of creating a sustained movement. These efforts failed. There was no movement resurgence, or at least no resurgence of a recognizable national movement. Some people looked for someone to blame for the failure. But with the advantage of historical distance, it seems unlikely that a new movement could have been built on its base. In retrospect, the Jena campaign was the last big protest that followed the Black solidarity script centering on Civil Rights organizations. Something different was going to be the basis for the next movement wave.

C. Gibson and Williams (2020) argue that the Jena campaign was the opening moment for the new round of Black organizing that later led to the Black Lives Movement. The young people inspired by the Jena mobilization became part of the next generation of activists. As Cathy Cohen argued, the next generation's activism would take different forms and create new organizations. Our study is focused on 2007, not on what happened later. Sources at the time mentioned revitalization of local organizing in many places. We know that a great deal of energy went into the Obama campaign and that during the Obama years there was an extensive infrastructure of training and support for organizing that became some of the underpinnings of the Black Lives Movement (Oliver 2020).

But nearly twenty years later, the lessons to be drawn from the mundane organizing version of the Jena 6 story are still valid. There are communities and networks of activists that are paying attention to cases that need action, as well as thinking about how to build their movements. The terrain is uncertain. The ordinary actions of trying to build support for specific causes and trying to build movement capacity sometimes succeed, and it is not possible to know in advance whether a given action will succeed or fail. The outcomes of mobilization efforts depend not only on activists' own actions but on the actions of others and larger contextual factors activists do not control. There will be opposition and counter-movements and failures as well as successes. If activists are there and have a community and a communications infrastructure that has the capacity for collective action, when the moment comes, they will be ready for it. And when that moment is over, it may have indirect consequences that are only apparent years later.

References

Abell, Peter. 2004. "Narrative Explanation: An Alternative to Variable-Centered Explanation?" *Annual Review of Sociology* 30 (1): 287–310. http://arjour nals.annualreviews.org/doi/abs/10.1146/annurev.soc.29.010202.100113.

Alexander, Michelle. 2010. *The New Jim Crow: Mass Incarceration in the Age of Colorblindness*. New York: New Press.

Barr, John, and Nicole Noren. 2007. "—OTL: 'Jena Six' Storm Involves Football Star." *ESPN.com*. www.espn.com/espn/news/story?id=3030458.

Bean, Alan. 2009. "Tulia and Jena: America in Miniature." *Sojourners* (blog). 2/17/2009. https://sojo.net/articles/tulia-and-jena-america-miniature.

———. 2010. "Interview with Alan Bean." Interviewed By Candice Ellis, Mike Brandon and Amanda Noll. 9/22/2010 *Samuel Proctor Oral History Program*. University of Florida MFP 071 Alan Bean 9–22–2010.

Berry, Jeffrey M., and Sarah Sobieraj. 2011. "Understanding the Rise of Talk Radio." *PS: Political Science & Politics* 44 (4): 762–767. https://dx.doi .org/10.1017/s1049096511001223.

Bob, Clifford. 2002. "Political Process Theory and Transnational Movements: Dialectics of Protest among Nigeria's Ogoni Minority." *Social Problems* 49 (3): 395–415.

Boutcher, Steven A. 2013. "Lawyering For Social Change: Pro Bono Publico, Cause Lawyering, And The Social Movement Society." *Mobilization* 18 (2): 179–196.

Brewer, Rose M. 2003. "Black Radical Theory and Practice: Gender, Race, and Class." *Socialism and Democracy* 17 (1): 109–122. https://doi.org/ 10.1080/08854300308428344.

Burch, Traci. 2023. *Which Lives Matter?: Factors Shaping Public Attention to and Protest of Officer-Involved Killings*. Cambridge: Cambridge University Press.

Burke, Jordan C. 2020. "White Discipline, Black Rebellion: A History of American Race Riots from Emancipation to the War on Drugs." PhD, University of New Hampshire (28262213).

BYP100. 2018. "About BYP 100." Accessed October 21, 2018. https://byp100 .org/about-byp100/.

Cha-Jua, SundiataKeita, and Clarence Lang. 2007. "The "Long Movement" as Vampire: Temporal and Spatial Fallacies in Recent Black Freedom Studies." *The Journal of African American History* 92 (2): 265–288. https://browzine.com/articles/194801402.

Chicago Citizen. 2006. "Should Illegal Immigrants Deserve Better Treatment than Blacks?" *Chicago Citizen*, March 5, 2006.

Christie, Raquel. 2008. "Double Whammy: It Took an Awfully Long Time for the National Media to Catch up to the Racial Turmoil in Jena, Louisiana. When They Did, the Results Were Not Exactly a Clinic in Precision Journalism." *American Journalism Review* 30: 16–25.

Cohen, Cathy J. 2010. *Democracy Remixed: Black Youth and the Future of American Politics*. Oxford: Oxford University Press, Incorporated.

Cole, Hazel Bell James. 2008. "'George Bush Doesn't Care About Black People': Hip Hop, Public Discourse and Black Politics in the Early 21st Century." PhD, The University of Southern Mississippi (3346523).

Couto, Richard A. 1993. "Narrative, Free Space, and Political Leadership in Social Movements." *Journal of Politics* 55 (1): 57–79.

Current, Gloster B. 1988. "The Significance of the N.A.A.C.P. and its Impact in the 1960s." *The Black Scholar* 19 (1): 9–18. https://doi.org/10.1080/00064246.1988.11412795.

DeRienzo, Paul. 2007. "Tony Brown and the Jena 6." September 23, 2007. Accessed January 22, 2023/22:01:06. www.youtube.com/watch?v=cVOq-p72vO4.

di Leonardo, Micaela. 2012. "Grown Folks Radio: U.S. Election Politics and a 'Hidden' Black Counterpublic." *American Ethnologist* 39 (4): 661–672. https://anthrosource.onlinelibrary.wiley.com/doi/abs/10.1111/j.1548-1425.2012.01386.x.

Djourelova, Milena, Ruben Durante, and Gregory J. Martin. 2025. "The Impact of Online Competition on Local Newspapers: Evidence from the Introduction of Craigslist." *Review of Economic Studies* 92 (3): 1738–1772. https://dx.doi.org/10.1093/restud/rdae049.

Donica, Karina. 2007. "Sharpton Learned of 'Jena Six' Case About 4 Week Ago." *The Town Talk*, August 7, 2007, A.1, News. Accessed January 22, 2023/14:52:05.

Ehrhardt, George. 2020. "Local Leaders in National Social Movements: The Tea Party." *Social Movement Studies* 19 (4): 373–390.

Emerson, Michael O., and Christian Smith. 2001. *Divided by Faith: Evangelical Religion and the Problem of Race in America*. New York: Oxford University Press.

Faison, Heather. 2008. "BLOGGER NATION." *Philadelphia Tribune*, June 4, 2008.

Fears, Darryl, Avis Thomas-Lester, and Washington Post Staff Writers. 2007. "Protesters to Converge on Louisiana Town; Black Teens' Case Resonates Nationally: [FINAL Edition]." *The Washington Post*, September 20, 2007.

Felber, Garrett. 2020. *Those Who Know Don't Say: The Nation of Islam, the Black Freedom Movement, and the Carceral State*. Chapel Hill: University of North Carolina Press.

Fine, Gary Alan. 1995. "Public Narration and Group Culture: Discerning Discourse in Social Movements." In *Social Movements and Culture*, edited by Hank Johnston and Bert Klandermans, 127–143. Minneapolis, MN: U of Minnesota Press.

Flaherty, Jordan. 2007a. "Justice in Jena." *Left Turn: Notes from the Global Intifada*, May 9, 2007, 2007a. Accessed January 22, 2023/22:29:08. https://web.archive.org/web/20071011212346/http://leftturn.mayfirst.org/?q=node%2F649.

2007b. "A matter of colour." *Morning Star Online*, August 15, 2007, 2007b. Accessed January 22, 2023/13:42:43.

2010. *Floodlines: Community and resistance from Katrina to the Jena Six (Kindle Edition)*. Haymarket Books.

Florini, Sarah. 2012. "Remembering the Past, Reframing the Present: Alternative Media and the Mnemonic Work of the Malcolm X Grassroots Movement." PhD, Indiana University (3527730).

2014. "Recontextualizing the Racial Present: Intertextuality and the Politics of Online Remembering." *Critical Studies in Media Communication* 31 (4): 314–326. https://doi.org/10.1080/15295036.2013.878028.

Foster, Mary. 2011. "5 Years Later, Jena 6 Move On." *NBC News*, August 25, 2011, 2011. Accessed January 22, 2023/19:15:09. www.nbcnews.com/id/wbna44275022.

Franklin, Craig. 2007. "Media Myths About the Jena 6." *Christian Science Monitor*, October 24, 2007. Accessed January 22, 2023/22:27:44. www.csmonitor.com/2007/1024/p09s01-coop.html.

Friedman, Eli. 2009. "External Pressure And Local Mobilization: Transnational Activism and the Emergence of the Chinese Labor Movement." *Mobilization* 14 (2): 199–218.

Fujino, Diane, and Matef Harmachis, eds. 2020. *Black Power Afterlives: The Enduring Significance of the Black Panther Party*. Chicago, IL: Haymarket Books.

Gamson, William A. 1995. "Constructing Social Protest." In *Social Movements and Culture*, edited by Hank Johnston and Bert Klandermans, 85–106. Minneapolis, MN: University of Minnesota Press.

Gibson, Camille, and Fay Williams. 2020. "Understanding the Impetus for Modern Student Activism for Justice at an HBCU: A Look at Personal Motivations." *The Urban Review* 52 (2): 263–276. https://doi.org/10.1007/s11256-019-00527-0.

Gibson, Dawn-Marie. 2012. *A History of the Nation of Islam: Race, Islam, and the Quest for Freedom*. Santa Barbara, CA: Praeger.

Goodman, Amy. 2007. "Hundreds March in Jena, Louisiana in Support of the Jena Six | Democracy Now!" *Democracy Now!*, January 8, 2007. Accessed May 30, 2025/19:21:44. www.democracynow.org/2007/8/1/hundreds_march_in_jena_louisiana_in.

Goodwyn, Wade. 2008. "Relentless Activist Digs into Racial Controversies." *NPR*, May 1, 2008/T08:00:00–05:00. www.npr.org/2008/01/05/17869393/relentless-activist-digs-into-racial-controversies.

Greenlea, Stephanie. 2014. "Free the Jena Six! Racism and the Circuitry of Black Solidarity in the Digital Age." PhD, Yale University (3580699).

Harris-Perry, Melissa V. 2011. *Sister Citizen: Shame, Stereotypes, and Black Women in America*. Yale University Press.

"Jena Six Case | C-SPAN.org." 2007. *C-SPAN.org* (10/16/2007). Accessed November 13, 2024/22:46:23. www.c-span.org/video/?201553-1/jena-case.

Johnson, Cedric. 2007. *Revolutionaries to Race Leaders Black Power and the Making of African American Politics*. Minneapolis: University of Minnesota Press, c2007.

Kane, Eugene. 2007. "EUGENE KANE; IN MY OPINION; Tales of Injustice Find Audiences via Internet." *Milwaukee Journal Sentinel*, February 9, 2007, B.3, News. Accessed January 22, 2023/15:51:23.

Kelley, Blair Murphy. 2010. *Right to Ride: Streetcar Boycotts and African American Citizenship in the Era of Plessy v. Ferguson*. Chapel Hill: The University of North Carolina Press.

Kelley, Robin D. G. 2015. *Hammer and Hoe: Alabama Communists during the Great Depression*. Twenty-fifth anniversary edition / with a new preface by the author. Chapel Hill: University of North Carolina Press.

Kovach, Gretel C., and Arian Campo-Flores. 2007. "A Town in Turmoil." *Newsweek* 150 (8/9): 36–38.

Lawrence, Regina G. 2000. *The Politics of Force: Media and the Construction of Police Brutality*. Berkeley: University of California Press, ©2000.

Lawson, Steven F. 2014. *Running for Freedom: Civil Rights and Black Politics in America Since 1941*. Hoboken: John Wiley & Sons, Incorporated.

Lester, Darryl Fears, and Avis Thomas. 2007. "Louisiana Case Stirs Outcry of Race Bias; Throngs to Protest Teens' Prosecution." *The Boston Globe*, September 20, 2007.

Lu, Todd. 2024. "When Black Movements Matter: Controlling Images And Black Lives Matter Protests In Media Attention To U.S. Police Killings." *Mobilization: An International Quarterly* 29 (1): 19–40. https://doi.org/10.17813/1086-671X-29-1-19.

Mangold, Tom. 2007a. "Racism goes on trial again in America's Deep South." *The Tennessee Tribune*, May 31–June 6, 2007, 2007a, 1.

2007b. "Racism goes on trial again in America's Deep South." *The Guardian*, September 20, 2007, 2007b. www.theguardian.com/world/2007/may/20/usa.theobserver.

2007c. "Racism Goes on Trial Again in America's Deep South: The Prosecution of Three Black Louisiana Youths Reveals the Rise of Discrimination by Stealth." *The Observer*, May 20, 2007/, 2007c, Observer Foreign Pages. Accessed January 22, 2023/13:18:38.

Marable, Manning. 2007. *Race, Reform, and Rebellion: The Second Reconstruction and beyond in Black America, 1945–2006*. 3rd ed. Jackson: University Press of Mississippi [Kindle edition].

Marquez, Benjamin author. 2021. *The Politics of Patronage: Lawyers, Philanthropy, and the Mexican American Legal Defense and Educational Fund*. 1st ed. Austin: University of Texas Press.

Mayer, William G. 2004. "Why Talk Radio Is Conservative." *Public Interest* 156: 86–103.

McCoy, Reginald. 2007. "Listen to me for a minute: Racial Tension in a Small Louisiana Town." *Listen to Me for a Minute* (blog). http://listentomeforaminute.blogspot.com/2007/04/racial-tension-in-small-louisiana-town.html.

Meyer, David S. 2006. "Claiming Credit: Stories of Movement Influence as Outcomes." *Mobilization: An International Journal* 11 (3): 201–218.

Minchin, Timothy J. 2008. "Making Best Use of the New Laws: The NAACP and the Fight for Civil Rights in the South, 1965–1975." *The Journal of Southern History* 74 (3): 669–702. www.jstor.org/stable/27650232.

Morant, Kesha M. 2008. "African-American Communication: The Continuity and Extension through Talk Elements of Commercial Black Radio." PhD, Howard University (3307747).

Morris, Aldon D. 1984. *The Origins of the Civil Rights Movement: Black Communities Organizing for Change*. New York, London: Free Press; Collier Macmillan.

Mort, Sébastien. 2012. "Tailoring Dissent on the Airwaves: The Role of Conservative Talk Radio in the Right-Wing Resurgence of 2010." *New*

Political Science 34 (4): 485–505. https://doi.org/10.1080/ 07393148.2012.729739.

Muhammad, Jesse. 2007. "Young Black Males the Target of Small-Town Racism." *Final Call.* www.finalcall.com/artman/publish/National_News_2/ Young_Black_males_the_target_of_small-town_racism_3753.shtml.

Musgrove, George Derek. 2019. "'There Is No New Black Panther Party': The Panther-Like Formations and the Black Power Resurgence of the 1990s." *The Journal of African American History* 104 (4): 619–656. www.journals .uchicago.edu/doi/abs/10.1086/705022.

NAACP. 2007. "NAACP Resolutions. 2007. Submitted under Article X, Section 2 of the Constitution of the NAACP." https://naacp.org/sites/ default/files/documents/Resolutions%202007_final.pdf.

Nichter, Matthew F. 2014. "Rethinking the Origins of the Civil Rights Movement: Radicals, Repression, and the Black Freedom Struggle." PhD, The University of Wisconsin – Madison (3668989).

2021. "'Did Emmett Till Die in Vain? Organized Labor Says No!': The United Packinghouse Workers and Civil Rights Unionism in the Mid-1950s." *Labor* 18 (2): 8–40. https://doi.org/10.1215/15476715-8849556.

Oliver, Pamela. 2020. "Resisting Repression: The Black Lives Movement in Context." In *Racialized Protest and the State: Resistance and Repression in a Divided America*, edited by Hank Johnston and Pamela Oliver, 63–88. Oxford and New York: Routledge.

Oliver, Pamela, and Mark Furman. 1989. "Contradictions between National and Local Organizational Strength: The Case of the John Birch Society." *International Social Movement Research* 2: 155–177.

Oliver, Pamela, Chaeyoon Lim, Morgan Matthews, and Alex Hanna. 2022. "Black Protests in the United States, 1994–2010." *Sociological Science* 9 (May): 275–312.

Payne, Charles M. 1995. *I've Got the Light of Freedom: The Organizing Tradition and the Mississippi Freedom Struggle*. Berkeley, CA: University of California Press.

Payton, Fay Cobb, and Lynette Kvasny. 2012. "Considering the Political Roles of Black Talk Radio and the Afrosphere in Response to the Jena 6: Social Media and the Blogosphere." *Information Technology & People* 25 (1): 81–102.

Polletta, Francesca. 1998a. "Contending Stories: Narrative in Social Movements." *Qualitative Sociology* 21 (4): 419–446.

1998b. "'It Was Like a Fever …' Narrative and Identity in Social Protest." *Social Problems* 45 (2): 137–159.

Raeshun, Iris. 2007. "Black Teens Charged with Attempted Murder in Louisiana." *Crisis, The*, September 1, 2007, 2007, UP FRONT. Accessed January 22, 2023/13:31:10.

Rahman, Ahmad A. 1996. "The Million Man March: A Black Woodstock?" *The Black Scholar* 26 (1): 41–44. www.jstor.org/stable/41068625.

Ransby, Barbara. 2018. *Making All Black Lives Matter: Reimagining Freedom in the Twenty-First Century*. Oakland, CA: University of California Press.

Recorder. 2006. "We should take advantage of the political influence from mass demonstrations." *Recorder*, April 14, 2006.

Reuning, Kevin, and Lee Ann Banaszak. 2020. "Measuring Protest For Comparisons: Multidimensional Scaling Of Action, Message, And Community." *Mobilization: An International Quarterly* 25 (3): 339–363. https://doi.org/10.17813/1086-671X-25-3-339.

Richie, Beth. 2012. *Arrested Justice Black Women, Violence, and America's Prison Nation*. New York: New York University Press.

Robinson, Eugene. 2007. "Drive Time for the 'Jena 6': [FINAL Edition]." *The Washington Post*, September 21, 2007.

Robnett, Belinda. 1997. *How Long? How Long?: African American Women in the Struggle for Civil Rights*. Cary: Oxford University Press, Incorporated.

——— 2020. "Defensive Adaptations: NAACP Responses to the US Post-Racial Project 1970–1990." In *Racialized Protest and the State*, edited by Hank Johnston and Pamela Oliver, 26–62. Oxford and New York: Routledge.

Rootes, Christopher. 2013. "From Local Conflict to National Issue: When and How Environmental Campaigns Succeed in Transcending the Local." *Environmental Politics* 22 (1): 95–114. https://doi.org/10.1080/09644016.2013.755791.

Rothman, Franklin Daniel, and Pamela E. Oliver. 1999. "From Local to Global: The Anti-Dam Movement in Southern Brazil, 1979–1992." *Mobilization* 4 (1): 41–57.

Shabazz, Saeed. 2007. "Sharpton & MLK III Rally for Jena Six." *New York Amsterdam News*, August 16–August 22, 2007, 4.

Simpson, Chaniqua D., Avery Walter, and Kim Ebert. 2021."'Brainwashing For The Right Reasons With The Right Message': Ideology And Political Subjectivity In Black Organizing." *Mobilization: An International Quarterly* 26 (4): 401–420. https://doi.org/10.17813/1086-671X-26-4-401.

Spencer, DeShuna. 2007. "NAACP at Forefront of Jena Six Case." *Crisis (15591573)* 114 (6): 41–42.

Stillerman, Joel. 2020. The Negro Labor Committee and the Dilemmas of Black Trade Unionism in New York City, 1925–1950. *SocArXiv*. https://doi.org/ https://doi.org/10.31235/osf.io/3hq86.

Taylor, James Lance. 2015. *Black Nationalism in the United States: From Malcolm X to Barack Obama*. Paperback edition. Boulder, CO: Lynne Rienner Publishers.

Taylor, Keeanga-Yamahtta. 2016. *From #BlackLivesMatter to Black Liberation*. Chicago, IL: Haymarket Books.

Thompson, Eddie. 2006. "The Battle Against Racism In Jena, Louisiana." *AuthorsDen.com* (blog). www.authorsden.com/visit/viewarticle.asp? id=25922&AuthorID=17296.

2007a. "The Battle Against Racism In Jena Hi-jacked." *AuthorsDen.com*. www.authorsden.com/visit/viewarticle.asp?id=29987&AuthorID=17296.

2007b. "The Battle Against Racism In Jena: Carpetbaggers and The Jena Six." *AuthorsDen.com*. www.authorsden.com/visit/viewarticle.asp? id=28358&AuthorID=17296.

Tyree, Tia C. M., and Melvin L. Williams. 2024. "Symposium Guest Editors' Introduction: Acknowledging the Historical and Contemporary Impact of Black Radio." *Journal of Radio & Audio Media* 31 (1): 7–11. https://dx .doi.org/10.1080/19376529.2024.2347793.

Vanderkooy, Patricia, and Stephanie J. Nawyn. 2011. "Identifying the Battle Lines: Local-National Tensions in Organizing for Comprehensive Immigration Reform." *American Behavioral Scientist* 55 (9): 1267–1286. https://journals.sagepub.com/doi/abs/10.1177/0002764211407838.

Voss, Kim, and Michelle Williams. 2012. "The Local in the Global: Rethinking Social Movements in the New Millennium." *Democratization* 19 (2): 352–377. https://dx.doi.org/10.1080/13510347.2011.605994.

Waldman, Amy. 2008. "The Truth About Jena." *The Atlantic*. www.theatlantic .com/magazine/archive/2008/01/the-truth-about-jena/306580/.

Waldron, Clarence, and Kevin Chappell. 2007. "Blacks Cry For Justice In Louisiana Town Rocked By High School Racial Violence." *Jet* 112 (7): 5–7.

Washington Informer. 2007. "NAACP Lends Its Support to 'Jena 6'." Washington Informer, July 26, 2007: 21.

Weddington, George. 2022. "Becoming Black Lives Matter: Racial Change and the Emergence of Black Movements." University of Pittsburgh PhD Dissertation. http://d-scholarship.pitt.edu/43462/.

2024. "Black Lives Matter and Recovering Black Occupy." American Sociological Association Collective Behavior and Social Movements Symposium, Online, May 17, 2024.

White, Lamar. 2006. "Open Thread: What the Heck Is Happening in Jena?" *CenLamar* (blog). December 12, 2006. https://cenlamar.com/2006/12/12/open-thread-what-the-heck-is-happening-in-jena/.

2007. "If you checked all the cars at the high school, you would find a lot more guns." *CenLamar* (blog). https://cenlamar.com/2007/05/12/if-you-checked-all-the-cars-at-the-high-school-you-would-find-a-lot-more-guns/.

Williams, Rhonda Y. 2015. *Concrete Demands: The Search for Black Power in the 20th Century.* New York: Routledge.

Witt, Howard. 2007a. "Bloggers inspire new civil rights wave; Jena 6 protest nurtured on Web: [Chicago Edition]." *Chicago Tribune*, September 19, 2007, 2007a, 1.1, News. Accessed June 13, 2024/13:15:23.

2007b. "Girl in prison for shove gets released early." *Chicago Tribune*, March 31, 2007, 2007b. Accessed June 10, 2023/13:02:08. www.chicagotribune.com/nation-world/chi-0703310265mar31-story.html.

Acknowledgments

This work derives from a larger project funded by the National Science Foundation grants SES1423784, SES 1918342, and SES2214160; and by the Wisconsin Alumni Research Foundation. Past research assistance by Morgan Matthews, John Lemke, and David Skalinder contributed to the larger project.

For EU product safety concerns, contact us at Calle de José Abascal, 56–1°,
28003 Madrid, Spain or eugpsr@cambridge.org.